ADVENTURES
OF
THE ELEMENTS

Richard E. James III

Illustrated By Tammy Isfeld

Embassy Court Productions

Library of Congress
Catalog Card No. 97-92928

ISBN: 1-57579-056-4

Published by
EMBASSY COURT PRODUCTIONS

Printed in United States of America

PINE HILL PRESS, INC.
Freeman, S. Dak. 57029

These adventures are dedicated to my family, especially my siblings who were inspirational in the character development. May one's imagination and dreams never be stifled by physical barriers or by scientific fact. Rather, may one thrive in the mystical aura of science and technology as it propels their imagination and dreams to unparalleled heights.

Episode One
Sunglasses ?

The crash of the screen door shattered the silence of the crisp autumn morning. A lively, young girl dashed into the backyard joining her ten year-old sister, Catherine. Absorbed in digging a hole for her magnolia tree, Catherine ignored the inquisitive stare of her younger sibling. Pausing for a moment, she excitedly gazed into the hole she had shoveled. A bright yellow butterfly drifted over the nearby hedge and settled upon a bud of the slender magnolia tree propped against a dented, tin pail.

"What ya looking at?" asked Jeanne-Marie, peering into the twelve-inch hole which for a four year-old looked very deep.

"I don't know. It looks like the top of a box but I can't pry it loose," said Catherine, masking her excitement.

"I'll get Richard. He can do it," said Jeanne-Marie, racing towards the house. Catherine watched her sister enter their two-story, white wood frame house slamming the screen door behind her. Dropping her shovel onto the closely cropped grass lawn, Catherine wondered why she always had to get her brothers before she could ever do anything.

Climbing into her older brother's bed, Jeanne-Marie began shouting, "Richard, Richie, wake up. Wake up. Catherine found a box... in a hole... in the yard."

Obviously annoyed at being awakened at an unusually early hour for a Saturday morning, Richard rolled over

1

and covered his head with the blankets in an attempt to shield himself from the constant pouncing of his younger sister. However, that last phrase, Catherine found a box, drew his attention. Reluctantly, Richard rolled out of bed dragging Jeanne-Marie with him.

"Hurry up. Come quickly," urged Jeanne-Marie, tugging her brother's arm.

"One second Jeanne-Marie, I'm sure the box isn't going to run away if it's been buried in the yard for this long," said Richard, wrinkling his brow in irritation.

All the excitement attracted Jacqueline who at the age of seven was intellectually quite advanced. With a book in one hand and her Christmas mouse in the other, Jacqueline brushed her long, strawberry blond locks out of her face and quizzically stared at Jeanne-Marie. "What's all the shouting about?" asked Jacqueline, placing her book and mouse upon her brother's bed.

"Catherine found a box," blurted Jeanne-Marie, "I'll get Anthony. He can help too," said Jeanne-Marie, darting down the narrow hallway with her long dark strands of hair trailing after her.

A hush fell over the five brothers and sisters as they encircled the tiny cavity in the yard. Solemnly Richard, the oldest of the children, grabbed the shovel and with a great heave hoisted the small box from the hole. The box was nothing more than a tattered dull, gray oaken container with two tiny, rusty hinges on one side and a bronze latch on the other. The gray paint easily flaked away as Anthony brushed the dirt from the top of the box. There was no lock.

"Open it Anthony," squealed Jeanne-Marie.

"I'll let Catherine open it since she found it," said Anthony, uncharacteristically displaying a sharing attitude.

"Err ... thanks," replied Catherine, a little shocked at her brother's kindness. She could only think he must be doing some early preparation to earn a spot on Santa's 'good boy' list for Christmas. With her head held high, Catherine snapped open the latch and slowly raised the lid of the small box.

"Sunglasses," said Jacqueline, disappointedly staring at several pairs of strangely decorated glasses.

"Put 'em on," shrieked Jeanne-Marie, grabbing for a pair of the bizarre looking, dark tinted glasses.

"Don't touch them," scolded Anthony, "we don't know who they belong to or where they've been."

"You worry too much," retorted Jacqueline, slipping on a purple pair of the strangely decorated glasses. "Wow."

"What is it? What do you see?" asked Richard. Each of the children snatched one of the five remaining pairs of glasses from the box.

"Oooo... What are they?" asked Catherine, gazing through her green spectacles. She never before saw anything like this: two blobs emerged appearing almost human in shape but not quite. The first creature, a bluish fellow with an enormous white O upon his chest, was no larger than a honeydew melon with two tiny arms and legs and a small round head. In fact, he looked much like a walnut with arms and legs. The miniature specimen wore a pint-size cape that looked as though it could cover his entire body.

Floating before the children, O's companion was similar in shape and could have easily been confused with his partner were it not for the large cyan colored N upon his chest. N gazed upon the children with a curious expression as if to say how absurd these large skinny creatures looked in their funny glasses. Peering at the children through two Lilliputian eyes sparkling in an almost mystical dance, N and O smiled from what should have been ear to ear; except for the fact, they had no visible ears.

"Hello there," greeted O cheerfully. Startled, Catherine, losing her balance, stumbled into the hole from which had come the magical sun glasses and crashed into the nearby hedge entangling her long, red hair in the branches.

"Are you ok, Catherine? I didn't mean to frighten you," said O. The two creatures danced merrily about the children. N chuckled gleefully as the bewildered children continued to stare with gaping mouths.

"How ... how do you know my name?" stammered Catherine, pulling twigs and leaves from her hair.

"That's easy. I've always been here. You couldn't see me until you put on the element glasses. By the way, you'll have to excuse my friend here. He always laughs at everything. He likes to pull pranks too but he means no harm by it," replied O, patting N on the head.

"Element glasses?" asked Jacqueline.

"Yes, element glasses. Oh, I'm sorry. I haven't formally introduced myself. I'm an element. In fact, I'm oxygen, the element you breathe which is exactly what you'll do to me if Richard and Anthony don't close their mouths," said Oxygen, giggling. "My friends call me Ollie Oxygen and this is Ned Nitrogen. I guess I'd better tell you about those glasses you're wearing and what they mean to you," said Ollie, straightening his cape.

4

"Aren't you too big for me to swallow?" asked Richard, adjusting his glasses.

"Yes, you don't have to worry about swallowing me. The oxygen atoms or elements you breathe are much smaller than me. In fact, they are too small for you to see. I'm the guardian of oxygen and Ned is the guardian of nitrogen which makes you human guardians."

"Human guardians? Elements? I don't understand. What's nit ... uhh ... nitrogen? I'm confused," cried Jeanne-Marie, tightly gripping Anthony's hand.

"Don't worry little one. We'll help you," said Ned, no longer laughing; but rather, attempting to comfort Jeanne-Marie who tried to hide behind her brother's leg.

"Yes, we'll help you and in turn you can help us," said Ollie, clumsily tripping over his cape while attempting to dry Jeanne-Marie's tears causing her to laugh.

"Basically, there are 109 element guardians that protect the elements to keep them from disappearing. Because, as you know, you can't survive without oxygen to breathe and even nitrogen makes up parts of you," stated Ned in his most serious sounding voice while straightening himself as tall as his plump little stomach would allow.

Ollie gently poked Ned in the belly causing him to exhale sharply and to shrink to his original stubby self. Chuckling softly, Ollie winked at Catherine who at this point wasn't sure as to whether or not she was dreaming. "The problem is that some of the guardians and even some humans that use elements have become evil. All elements can make or do good things but they can also cause destruction or harm if they land in the wrong hands."

"That's where we need you're help," said Ned, smiling at the stunned group of children. "As long as you wear the glasses you will be able to see and to talk to us."

"It's your choice; but, if you decide not to help, please place the element glasses in the box and..."

"We'd love to help," said Richard. The other four children nodded in agreement. "But who is the extra pair of glasses for?" asked Richard, gently lifting them from the box.

"Oh, that's in case a pair gets broken or in case another is chosen as a guardian," said Ned. "Keep them in a safe place for now."

"What's that big letter on your tummy?" sniffled Jeanne-Marie, appearing to be feeling much better now.

"Aahhh, that's my ... let's see ... what do your scientist call it? Oh yes, that's my chemical symbol. My letter is N for nitrogen and Ollie's is O for oxygen. Let me introduce you to a few more of our friends who protect the little elements that make up the rest of the air around you. Then we'll tell you about our latest problem or as we guardians like to say, adventure," stated Ned proudly. Silently slipping behind Ollie, he untied his blue companion's cape. Roaring with laughter, Ned darted upwards as Ollie frantically scrambled to grab his cloak.

With cheeks rosy red from blushing, after feeling a bit breezy without his cape, Ollie Oxygen addressed the children. "If you will look upwards to where my foolish friend has fled, you'll see the seven other guardians of the elements needed to create earth's air."

"Hi," sang a chorus of voices, greeting the children staring into the clear autumn sky.

6

A rather chubby element with a large X and a small e upon his stomach plopped upon Jacqueline's shoulder. This peculiar individual, Xe, wore a strange, tiny green hat on his head and appeared much too large for his cape. He too, like the remaining six elements, was blue in color.

In a kingly voice ringing joyously through the crisp air, Xe proclaimed, "Nice to make your acquaintance. I am Xerxes Xenon, pronounced *ZURK-seez Zee-nahn*, even though I spell it X-e-r-x-e-s X-e-n-o-n. I am the guardian of xenon elements. Even though xenon only makes up a very small part of air, it is used in making very powerful lamps. I shall quickly introduce you to the other six air elements who you will meet more closely at a later date," said Xerxes. Inhaling deeply, Xerxes attempted to rapidly rattle off the names of the remaining elements present. "To my left is Holly Hydrogen with the symbol H, next to her is Carl Carbon with the great big C who is here on a special assignment, and I'll tell you the rest of their names as soon as I catch my breath," gasped Xerxes Xenon, turning even bluer in the face than his original color.

"Wow, you didn't have to say all of that in one breath," said Catherine, who for the most part had been silent. "Why do you have such a funny looking hat on your head?" asked Catherine, quizzically staring at the plump little element.

As Ned Nitrogen erupted in uproarious laughter, Xerxes Xenon glared at Catherine. "Young lady, how dare you call this a funny looking hat. Why, this is a nobleman's crown fit for a king."

"I'm sorry," said Catherine, shocked by Xerxes outburst. "I didn't mean to upset you. Are you some type of a king?"

"Apology accepted," replied Xerxes, centering his hat upon the top of his little round head. "As a matter of fact, I am a king, a nobleman to be more exact. Even my first name, Xerxes, is the name of a king. I should have you know that Xerxes was once the powerful king of the ancient civilization of Persia, which is now the country of Iran; but, that's enough of a history lesson for today." Clambering to his feet, Xerxes Xenon began strutting about Jacqueline's head. "If you look closely, you will see that Henry Helium (He), Nelson Neon (Ne), Arla Argon (Ar), and Kris Krypton (Kr) also wear the noble crowns. There is one other element, Randal Radon who has the symbol Rn, who likewise possesses the distinguished honor of wearing this crown. Unfortunately, Randal Radon couldn't be here at the moment," said Xerxes, indignantly watching Jeanne-Marie search under the nearby hedge for Randal. At the sight of Xerxes stern gaze, Catherine pulled her younger sister from under the hedge fearing something terrible might happen if they failed to give this strange element their undivided attention. "We six elements are officially known as the noble gases. All the others here are nothing more than your common elements," said Xerxes haughtily, appearing to Catherine to be quite confident of himself and his noble stature.

"Common," exclaimed a flustered Ned Nitrogen. Catherine wondered who wouldn't become flustered by Xerxes Xenon's pompous attitude. "We may be common but who is more important. You only make up part of one percent of air. I make up seventy-eight percent of air and oxygen makes up twenty-one percent of this air. You're only used in flash lamps while I'm used as fertilizer for plants and as liquid nitrogen to freeze food."

"I beg your pardon. I help to make bubble chambers. The very scientific instruments used by physicists to study nuclear particles," said Xerxes, angrily pacing about Jacqueline's head.

"Ha, that's it. I make up proteins which are the building blocks for all living organisms. Without me there would be no physicists to bother using you in making their instruments for science. In fact, there wouldn't even be any plants or animals," snarled Ned, shaking a little blue finger at Xerxes.

"Well Mr. common, ordinary Ned Nitrogen, that fertilizer of yours which doesn't get used by the plants ends up polluting the water and air. And on top of that..." scolded Xerxes, smugly folding his arms across the large Xe upon his chest.

"That's enough. What type of an example are you setting for the children, our future guardians," interrupted Ollie Oxygen. Catherine cautiously observed Ollie's disgust with the childish antics of his two fellow elements. "Let's get back to business and explain the problem at hand. These human guardians aren't going to wait all day to help us. You'll have to excuse these two," said Ollie, stepping between Ned and Xerxes.

As Xerxes Xenon stomped into the distance, that is stomping as well as one can stomp in the air, the younger of the two brothers spoke, "I want to hear about the adventure, but what's Carl Carbon's special assignment?"

"Anthony, that's just like you to ask another question when we're about to hear the elements' adventure," exclaimed Jacqueline impatiently.

"Patience my dear, all in good time," assured Ollie. "Unfortunately, Carl Carbon left to attend to some important tasks but I will briefly explain his assignment."

"Uuuuggghhh," sighed Jacqueline. Catherine giggled at the sight of her younger sister who appeared as if she would burst from all of the suspense.

Patting Jacqueline on the head, Ollie Oxygen attempted to comfort her. "My you sure are impatient. I'll make this quick. Basically, carbon can only be in the air when he is connected to two oxygens to form the molecule carbon dioxide. Basically, a molecule is just two or more elements connected together. And as you know, carbon dioxide is the molecule that you breathe out or exhale and that plants take in as they give off oxygen. I told you it was simple. Almost all elements can join together to form some type of molecule."

"Wow, that's just like in the cartoons when a bunch of machines join together to make bigger and different machines," said Catherine, peering closely at Ned impatiently twiddling his thumbs.

"That's right," agreed Ned Nitrogen, giggling uncontrollably "Quit breathing on me Catherine. It tickles," said Ned, laughingly wrapping himself in his cape.

"Oops, sorry," said Catherine, blushing.

Pausing for a moment to brush the wrinkles from his cape, Ollie gazed upon the children. "Without carbon dioxide, most plants would die and then who would make oxygen for you to breathe? Therefore, Carl Carbon is on a special assignment to assure that each carbon is being connected to two oxygens. If carbon is only connected with one oxygen, it creates the poisonous monstrous gas named Urban Carbon Monoxide. But enough of that, I don't want to bore you with the details. Urban..."

"Now for the adventure," interrupted Ned.

"I was just getting to that. If you wouldn't so rudely interrupt me," scolded Ollie. Catherine knew she was going to like Ollie especially after he playfully winked at Ned Nitrogen. It seemed nothing could upset Ollie Oxygen for long. "As I was about to say, this evil menace, Urban Carbon Monoxide, has lately been causing the element guardians quite a bit of trouble. We need your help in battling this fiend."

"What can we do?" asked Richard, flexing his muscles causing his brother and sisters to laugh.

"Well, you may be strong for a for a fifteen year-old, but I'm afraid it's going to take more than physical strength to defeat Urban Carbon Monoxide," warned Ollie Oxygen, gravely stroking his chin. "Oh my, look at the time, it's getting close to lunch. I don't want to keep you from the delicious, nutritious meal your mother prepared. We will begin the quest to defeat Urban Carbon Monoxide this afternoon. Take care of your glasses and don't let them slip into the wrong hands."

"We will," said Anthony, "but how will we find you?"

"Don't worry about that. Any time you wear your element glasses, Ollie or I and even sometimes his highness Xerxes Xenon will be here," said Ned Nitrogen, grabbing Xerxes hat and dashing into the distance.

"Aaaarrrghhh, you shall pay for your insolence, you simple commoner," growled Xerxes, chasing after Ned.

"See you later," said Ollie Oxygen, chuckling as he pursued the atomic trail left by the two fleeing atoms or elements as they call themselves. The five children stared with disbelief at what had occurred and slowly removed their element glasses placing them gently in the tattered gray box.

"Time for lunch," announced Jeanne-Marie, racing for the house as quickly as her little legs would carry her.

"Aaaahhh, I missed breakfast," groaned Richard. He and the other children dashed for the house eagerly awaiting the next time they would wear their element glasses to confront the sinister Urban Carbon Monoxide.

Episode Two
Urban Carbon Monoxide

The wind playfully tossed the orange, brown, and yellow leaves of autumn through the brisk sunny afternoon greeting five excited children racing towards an old dilapidated shack in a distant corner of a wooded lot. Glancing behind her as she entered the shack, Catherine couldn't help but notice how far she was from the house which looked like a tiny white speck on the horizon. She didn't always like venturing this far from the security of her home. The tallest of the children who appeared to be about thirteen removed a thin piece of plywood from the dirt floor of the wooden shack revealing a small hole. Reaching inside, he withdrew a tattered gray box with the word elements scrawled across the top of the oak container.

"Are we ready?" asked Anthony, slowly opening the box. "We don't know what we'll be getting into by agreeing to help those elements. That Ned Nitrogen looks a little suspicious to me."

"Ssshhhh, the elements are all around us and even though we can't see them; they can see and especially hear us," warned the older brother.

"Richard's right," agreed Jacqueline. "The air elements seem friendly," said Jacqueline, gazing at the numerous shovels, rakes, and other gardening tools strewn about the shed.

14

"Okay, we'll trust them for now. I'm sorry if I offended any elements," replied Anthony reluctantly. He and the other four children put on their element glasses and stared intently about the shack.

"Welcome back," greeted Ollie Oxygen. Catherine eagerly noted Ollie's usual cheerful demeanor. Hovering behind Ollie, Ned poked his tongue at Anthony.

Giving Anthony a wink, Ned declared, "I understand you not wanting to trust us. All of this can be hard to believe. Besides, it's not always easy to be friends with someone who looks so much different than you."

"But we're glad you're back," said Ollie. "Now let's tend to this business of Urban Carbon Monoxide."

"It's gotten worse than we thought. In fact, Urban Carbon Monoxide is headed this way right now. We don't have much time," cautioned Ned Nitrogen who Catherine noticed was no longer in a joking mood.

"Let me tell you a little about this terrible monster we'll be fighting. It's always good to know your opponent," said Ollie.

"But I don't want to fight anyone," cried Jeanne-Marie, tightly clutching her stuffed kangaroo.

"Don't worry. I'll handle all the punches," assured Richard. As Anthony nodded, Catherine rolled her eyes and wondered why boys always wanted to act tough. "We're ready for some action."

"Not too fast boys," warned Ollie Oxygen. "This carbon monoxide is a cunning villain."

"Let someone who is educated in the arts and history tell you about this Urban Carbon Monoxide," announced Xerxes Xenon, squeezing his chubby, stout body through a crack in the wood shingled roof of the shack.

"Oh, it's his majesty. Do tell us oh wise one," smirked Ned, bowing before Xerxes.

"Hmmfff," snorted Xerxes Xenon, slapping his little green hat firmly upon his smooth round head. "I'll ignore the pitiful tauntings of one as naive as Ned Nitrogen. Now children, Urban Carbon Monoxide at one time was good and he still could be good if he wasn't jealous of Di Carbon Dioxide, the guardian of carbon dioxide molecules."

"Jealous?" squeaked Jeanne-Marie, hugging her stuffed kangaroo too tightly causing the stuffing to make the kangaroo's head grow larger.

"Yes, jealous," said Xerxes, "Good carbon monoxide is used in fuel gases to heat homes and to cook food. However, Urban Carbon Monoxide began to notice how carbon dioxide was everywhere while his carbon monoxide only appeared in small amounts. This enraged Urban Carbon Monoxide who began scheming of ways to make more carbon monoxide in the hopes of exceeding the number of carbon dioxide molecules."

"What's wrong with having a bunch of carbon monoxide around anyway?" asked Catherine, observing the concerned expressions on the faces of the little elements.

"Aahhh my innocent child, carbon monoxide pollutes the air and is extremely poisonous to humans, plants, and animals," answered Xerxes Xenon.

"I'm getting confused with all this monoxide and dioxide stuff. Uugghhh, my brain hurts," exclaimed Catherine, becoming more baffled.

"Precisely, Urban Carbon Monoxide is a very sneaky, conniving demon. He wants you to be confused. First, he tried to make himself look as much like Di Carbon Dioxide as possible. They both have the letters CO on their

16

chest but Di has a little 2 after her CO because she has two oxygens connected to her carbon. Urban only has one oxygen connected with his carbon. This was another reason for Urban Carbon Monoxide to be jealous of Di because he could never have two oxygens at once. He was born with only one magical bond or connection for oxygen." Clearing his throat, Xerxes adjusted the green cape about his neck. "Since Urban could never make two oxygen's stick to him; he began taking oxygen and carbon elements as well as some carbon dioxide molecules prisoner. He then burns the carbon elements with either oxygen or carbon dioxide to create even more carbon monoxide. I hear it's dreadfully painful..."

"That's why the element guardian Carl Carbon has been busy. He's been trying to rescue the poor little carbon prisoners," interrupted Ollie Oxygen.

"Quite true," agreed Xerxes Xenon, "Now please have some respect and don't interrupt until I finish my lecture. Where was I? Oh yes, taking prisoners was not enough for Urban Carbon Monoxide. He even thought of ways to trick humans into making more carbon monoxide. Urban didn't care if it meant people and animals would die when they breathed too much of the poisonous carbon monoxide."

"How does he trick people?" asked Jacqueline. Catherine gently patted her sister on the arm realizing how frightened she was becoming.

"That's an easy trick. Every time someone drives a car, the engine burns gas and oil which creates carbon monoxide in deadly amounts. Some car makers have put parts in cars reducing the amount of carbon monoxide escaping into the air. However, it's not enough to stop the carbon monoxide. Even cigarette smoke makes small amounts of carbon monoxide," said Xerxes, pausing for a moment. Catherine could only assume this brief pause was a chance for Xerxes to gather his thoughts for another shower of facts. She never before met anyone who liked to talk as much as this plump blue fellow and was glad for the moment of silence. Actually, Catherine hoped he would never get his thoughts together and maybe then they could get to the point of the matter.

"How will we see him?" asked Richard who Catherine noticed no longer appeared eager for a fight.

"That is another one of his tricks," said Xerxes. "Urban Carbon Monoxide has no taste, no smell, and no color but with your element glasses you will see him. Even though Urban has tried to look like Di Carbon Dioxide, he has been evil for too long; and as a result, Urban Carbon Monoxide has grown twisted and ugly. He transformed into a dark purplish, skeleton rising from a thick mass of gas and is marked with a huge black CO across his chest. Urban is as tall as this ten foot shack and numerous smaller carbon monoxides ooze from the frayed cloak draping about his bony remains. A terrible scowl frowns from beneath two glowing, dagger-like eyes. No one has ever been able to see the rest of his facial features hidden beneath the shadow cast from the large brim of his hat. He is darkness and if you are fooled by his tricks, he will kill you. Not even our element powers can stop him for long."

"Waaaa," wailed Jeanne-Marie, trembling with fear.

"Wha ... what could we possibly do?" asked Catherine. Trying to remain brave for the sake of her younger sisters,

Catherine huddled closer to the other children and attempted to stop her thin arms and legs from trembling.

"We need you to help us rescue the carbon and oxygen elements trapped in Urban Carbon Monoxide's prison in the abandoned coal mine deeper in this forest. We have to also encourage the people around here to quit doing so many of the things that create carbon monoxide..." began Ollie Oxygen. A spine-tingling shriek sounded through the trees surrounding the shack causing a dreadful hush to fall over the group.

The roar of a nearby car engine revved into high gear breaking the momentary silence. Catherine moaned remembering her neighbor's awful habit of driving his car to get his morning paper at the end of his driveway. She especially hated cold mornings like this morning when her neighbor would let his car run endlessly to allow the heater to warm the interior of his vehicle before he drove it. *How ridiculous*, she thought. A sudden thump against the wooden wall of the shack forced everyone in the shed to hold their breath. Catherine stared in terror at the gnarled shack door which she observed was in dire need of a paint job. How Catherine wished she could be painting the door rather than fearing what may be on the other side of it. She gasped in horror as a white streak shot through the crack under the door. Exhaling sharply, Catherine realized it was only Carl Carbon.

"He's here. It's Urban Carbon Monoxide. Quickly, we have to get away from the shack. Grab the extra pair of element glasses. We can't let him get his wicked hands on them," declared Carl Carbon who to Catherine appeared to be unsuccessfully attempting to look courageous.

As the five children and four element guardians rushed for the shack door; an evil, black shadow crept through the holes and notches in the walls of the dilapidated building. Their only escape exit blocked by the hideous Urban Carbon Monoxide; the children cringed in fear.

"Get back," shouted Carl Carbon. "Urban is trying to fill the shack with his deadly carbon monoxide. There isn't much time before we run out of oxygen."

"Are we going to die," sobbed Jeanne-Marie, tearfully watching Richard and Anthony turn ghostly pale.

"We won't let that happen," assured Ollie Oxygen. "I can make extra oxygen until the carbon monoxide becomes overpowering," said Ollie, pointing his clenched fist towards the door. "By the power of the elements, let there be oxygen." A blue ray of light with bright white sparks shot forth from Ollie's hand. A gush of oxygen rich air rushed over the children forming a dark blue wall of oxygen in front of the shack door halting the progress of the black carbon monoxide. "That should hold for the moment," exclaimed Ollie.

"We have to shut off the car. It's only adding to Urban Carbon Monoxide's power," instructed Carl Carbon.

"I think we have enough air element guardians to make an air stream," said Ned Nitrogen. "It'll be a weak air stream since we don't have all of the element guardians who make up the air with us. None of the other element guardians will be able to get through Urban Carbon Monoxide's cloud of death. However, the majority of the air elements are with us especially since Ollie and I together make up ninety-nine percent of the air. Ollie, we're going to need you to use maximum power even though it will leave you very weak. Carbon monoxide can't continue to grow in oxygen rich air."

"I think it'll work. Excellent idea," said Xerxes Xenon who Catherine noticed at this particular moment didn't care that someone besides a noble gas had come up with the plan. "We should be able to create a tunnel of air through the Carbon Monoxide that will allow us to escape from this rickety cabin."

"We'll have to move quickly. It won't take long for Urban Carbon Monoxide to break through our fragile tunnel," warned Ned Nitrogen. "As soon as we've created the air tunnel, Richard run and stop the car. The rest of you follow Richard and we'll be right behind you," shouted Ned, pointing his fist towards the door.

"I summon the power of xenon," roared Xerxes Xenon, majestically shooting a brilliant green ray at the black smoke clouding the door.

"By the power of nitrogen, let there be air," screamed Ned Nitrogen, blasting a streak of blinding red light at the dark carbon monoxide.

"Carbon," roared Carl Carbon, firing a dazzling white stream of light which sparkled like a thousand diamonds.

"By the power of the elements, let there be oxygen," yelled Ollie Oxygen, pointing both fists toward the door. His glittering blue beams joined the other three elements' rays.

With a sudden flash, a blinding white tunnel with silvery streaks appeared. It not only sliced through the evil carbon monoxide but through the shack door as well. The five children froze, stunned by the marvel before their eyes.

"Go, go, run," yelled Carl, snapping the children to their senses.

Richard dashed through the tunnel followed by Jacqueline and Jeanne-Marie dragging her kangaroo after her. The mystical circular passage began to shimmer and shake as small dark lines trickled through the white lining of the tunnel. Emerging from the air stream, Richard glanced behind him to see Anthony, Catherine, and the three elements, struggling to carry Ollie, racing through the collapsing passageway.

"They're not going to make it," screamed Richard. The opening of the tunnel began to disintegrate; swallowed by the dark smoky cloud of Urban Carbon Monoxide. "I have to stop the car."

Turning and dashing for the driveway, Richard tripped and fell in the dry grass scattering leaves left and right. With precious seconds wasted, the red-haired fifteen year-old staggered to his feet. Sprinting towards the car, Richard witnessed a ghastly cloud of carbon monoxide, rising from the dark blue sedan, streaking to join the ranks of the hideous figure of Urban Carbon Monoxide. Panting heavily, the lanky teenager covered the final fifty yards seperating him from the vehicle. Struggling with the cumbersome door, Richard jerked it open and found the key in the ignition of the car. Quickly twisting his wrist, he silenced the horrible rumble of the engine; but, had he done it in time to weaken Urban Carbon Monoxide enough to prevent the tunnel from collapsing?

Glancing upward, Anthony could only watch the tunnel shake violently before all was still leaving behind an eery silence. Grabbing Catherine by the hand, Anthony and the elements made a final sprint for the exit of the passageway.

"Made it," gasped Ned, seconds before the black twisted shadow of Urban Carbon Monoxide completely engulfed the shack and tunnel. "Shutting off the car slowed Urban's growth just enough for us to make it through the tunnel. We did it," said Ned Nitrogen who Catherine noted was relieved to be in one piece.

"We're not out of danger yet," warned Xerxes Xenon. "Here he comes. Run for the woods. Wait, Catherine and Anthony go home and stop everyone from making such vast amounts of carbon monoxide. Don't worry, Urban Carbon Monoxide will follow us. He won't bother chasing you; he only wants to destroy the element guardians for now. There's a hole in the gas line leading to your stove that is leaking deadly amounts of carbon monoxide. I think Urban may have created the hole. Arla Argon will meet you there," said Xerxes, waving and rushing towards the edge of the woods.

Oozing past the shack, Urban Carbon Monoxide followed the elements and children into the dense vegetation of the thicket, dripping smaller rotten blobs of carbon monoxide after him.

"We've got to rescue the carbon and oxygen elements and the carbon dioxide molecules before Urban arrives at the abandoned coal mine and rebuilds his strength," said Ned.

"Why can't you use your element powers and destroy Urban Carbon Monoxide," asked Jacqueline, gasping for air as she ran along the forest path.

"We aren't powerful enough. Besides, he does serve a purpose in making other chemical molecules or compounds which we are too weak to help make. So he can do good," confessed Ollie, who to Richard looked rather weak after expending most of his energy on creating the air tunnel. "But, he has chosen the dark path and we must stop him. Unfortunately, Urban is a molecule made up of two elements, carbon and oxygen, joined in a magical bond. That allows him to have the power of more than one element."

"Yep, we are nothing more than simple elements, or atoms as some say even though I hate that word. It's too bland and ordinary. Element is a much more noble word with many more letters," chipped in Xerxes Xenon, gripping his hat to keep it from blowing away as he floated through the trees. "Our powers can stop a molecule for a short time; usually long enough for us to escape. But, molecules join their many element powers together to create mightier forces than we can."

"Fortunately, we elements can join our powers together to create molecules but it's very difficult," said Ned Nitrogen, catching a ride on Carl Carbon's sparkling white cape. "The only problem facing us is we must have the exact amount and type of elements needed to create the molecule we want. As you saw with the air tunnel; if we're lacking even part of the proper elements, then the molecule we create will be very weak or even nonexistent. There are some rare cases though where certain elements can defeat a molecule. Unfortunately, this isn't one of them."

"Weak indeed," chimed Xerxes Xenon, nimbly guiding his rather large belly through the branches of the trees. "Even if we do manage to create a perfect molecule, it only lasts for a short period. In addition, good elements can usually only create good molecules."

"What about Di Carbon Dioxide? She can help; can't she?" asked Jacqueline, continuing to run along the barely perceptible, narrow path twisting through the dense foliage.

"Yes, most definitely," answered Ollie Oxygen, who Richard noticed was growing more energetic. "The only problem is Di has her hands full keeping Urban's evil henchmen from capturing any more carbon dioxide molecules. Besides, she is denser than air and can't float about as easily as we or the ruthless Urban Carbon Monoxide can."

"Are you calling Di Carbon Dioxide dumb?" asked Ned angrily.

"No, you brainless atom," exclaimed Xerxes, glaring at Ned. "Ollie said she was dense. He means Di is heavy. Now don't get me wrong. I didn't say she was fat. Di Carbon Dioxide is simply heavier than air and therefore can't move very quickly. If she was here, she could easily contest Urban until he eludes her again. I doubt she will make it in time to help us though," said Xerxes Xenon. The small group climbed to the top of the ridge overlooking the abandoned coal mine.

"How are we going to get in there?" asked Richard, peering at two gelatinous beasts standing before the cave entrance. Each of the ghastly carbon monoxide warriors towered over the elements surrounding the children.

"No problem," answered Ned, smiling at the rejuvenated Ollie Oxygen. "Those henchmen are nothing more than overgrown carbon monoxide molecules. Granted, they are twice as large and stronger than normal elements and molecules but they lack the power of the guardians. If Ollie blasts them with enough oxygen, they will disintegrate."

"You bet," agreed Carl Carbon who had finally caught up with the group. Richard giggled softly realizing even though Carl was a nonmetal element, he wasn't quite as fast as the air elements which had disappointed Ned because it had forced him to quit hitching a free ride on Carl's cape.

"What took you so long?" squealed Jeanne-Marie. Richard knew his younger sister was thrilled to know she could finally run faster than somebody.

"Even though I can help form air molecules such as in creating the molecule carbon dioxide, I'm not an air element. That's why I'm not as fast as the elements who guard the chemical formula or secret code for air. Each molecule has a secret code or chemical formula showing how each of the elements fit together to create a particular molecule. Each element guardian knows his part of the chemical formula but doesn't always know the other elements' codes." Richard listened intently wishing he knew a secret chemical formula but realized he could never have the power of the elements. "I'm usually a diamond in my pure form but if I get hot enough, I become the carbon gas you see now," said Carl whose large C sparkled in the rays of sunlight peeking through the great limbs of the ancient oaks.

"Wow, you're a diamond," blurted Jacqueline. Shocked by his sister's sudden burst of energy especially after running through the woods, Richard wondered whether or not they would survive another of Urban Carbon Monoxide's deadly attacks. He wasn't too confident they'd have enough time to rescue the prisoners and escape before Urban returned. "That means you're harder than a rock and of course more beautiful."

"Well, thank you but I'm not in my solid form right now. A solid would go through a gas without causing it any harm. Besides, I work better as a guardian when I'm in my gaseous form..." said Carl cut short by a dreadful hush falling over the forest. The air grew thick with smoke heralding the approach of Urban Carbon Monoxide.

"He's coming," whispered Xerxes Xenon cautiously. "We'd better get moving."

The small band of elements and children slipped down the ridge and crept towards the entrance of the mine. A foul odor leaked from the cavernous opening. Bone-chilling screams echoed through the cave ominously greeting the terrified group drawing ever closer to the carbon monoxide henchmen.

"Oxygen," yelled Ollie, pointing a fist at each of the evil warriors. A dazzling blue beam shot from each of Ollie's clenched fists atomizing the carbon monoxides into microscopic particles.

"Behind you," shouted Ned, pointing at four more warriors rushing towards the mine firing thin streaks of black carbon monoxide.

"I summon the power of xenon," roared Xerxes, shooting a brilliant green ray at the foursome. Xerxes Xenon's beam exploded in front of the carbon monoxides momentarily blinding them.

"Good shot. I've got them," yelled Ollie, turning and rapidly blasting the hideous warriors into nothingness.

"Quickly, get inside," ordered Carl Carbon, leading the way into the dimly lit coal mine.

Back in the yard, two children could be seen racing towards a wood frame house.

"Run Catherine, we've got to stop the carbon monoxide from filling our house," yelled Anthony, bursting through the back door. The children's mother slumped at the kitchen table with her head in her hands feeling slightly dizzy from inhaling the carbon monoxide leaking from the stove.

"Mamma doesn't know the danger she's in," whispered Catherine, nervously wringing her hands. "She can't see the carbon monoxide or even smell it without our element glasses."

"I know," replied Anthony. The two children masking their fear entered the dining room.

"I'm glad you made it," greeted a soft voice. An element with a large pink Ar appeared before the children. She wore a pink hat closely resembling Xerxes Xenon's funny looking green hat. With a thin strip of lace attached to the bottom of her cape and a band of pink around her neck, she radiated an air of royalty. Otherwise, she looked like any of the other elements.

"You must be Arla Argon," said Catherine, excited to meet a noble female gas. "We saw you with the other air elements."

"That was me," replied Arla Argon, curtseying before Catherine. "I make up almost one percent of the air. In fact, I make up more of the air than the noble Xerxes Xenon," said Arla, laughing.

"Ned said you could help us," said Anthony. Catherine could sense her brother's displeasure realizing he was not quite sure a female element could do anything for them.

"Oh that Ned," giggled Arla Argon, "he and I are good friends. As a matter of fact, all of the light bulbs in your house are filled with argon and nitrogen elements. Without Ned Nitrogen and I, you wouldn't have any light bulbs."

"That's great," replied Anthony sarcastically, "but right now we've got more important things to worry about like our mom whose passed out on the table."

"How right you are young man," declared Arla Argon, no longer laughing. "Catherine turn off the stove and open the windows. We need to get as much fresh air as possible flowing through the house. Anthony and I will go outside and temporarily stop the leak. Get your dad and warn him and your mom about the danger. While your at it, tell your neighbor to quit driving his car to get his newspaper. He's making too much carbon monoxide and besides he can walk that far. He definitely could use the exercise."

As Catherine raced towards the kitchen, Anthony grabbed a roll of tape and joined Arla behind the house where a black cloud slowly oozed from a long galvanized pipe. The cloud of carbon monoxide trickled towards the dark trail left by Urban Carbon Monoxide. At the sight of Arla Argon, the cloud shrieked in terror and retreated.

"Why'd it do that?" asked Anthony, quite puzzled by the carbon monoxide's unusual behavior.

"Believe it or not, I can temporarily stop carbon monoxide," replied Arla Argon.

"You... you can?" stammered Anthony.

"Yes, I can form a protective shield capable of blocking oxygen and other gases."

"Why would you want to block oxygen?" asked Anthony, completely confused by this female element's powers.

"Well, when oxygen combines with metals, it can cause them to rust and tarnish which can be a very important process in nature. However, if you want to join two metals together, you don't want any oxygen causing rust between them. That's why I block the tiny oxygen's, who don't know the damage rust causes, until the two metals have been joined together usually by welding."

"Oh, ok," said Anthony, not sure he fully understood what Arla was explaining. "If you can block carbon monoxide, why don't you stop Urban Carbon Monoxide?"

"I wish I could," answered Arla Argon, gently tugging at the lace fringe on her cape. "Unfortunately, I'm just an element and my power will only stop the gas for a short period of time. As an element, I'm too weak to stop a molecule but we can at least fix this leak. Once I've sealed the pipe, you wrap it in tape." Anthony nodded in agreement. He was actually beginning to grow fond of this female noble gas. "I summon the power of Argon," yelled Arla. A blazing pink light shot forth from the palm of her hand forming a pink shield trapping the carbon monoxide in the pipe. Anthony quickly wrapped the pipe with tape and high-fived Arla Argon.

"Daddy's coming to fix the pipe and I told everyone about the dangers of making too much carbon monoxide," announced Catherine, jogging around the corner of the house.

"Great," said Arla Argon. "Let's catch up with the others."

Back in the coal mine, a small group cautiously advanced through the maze of tunnels wrinkling their noses in a futile attempt to block the stifling odor seeping from the numerous dark caverns. A great fire burned in the distance. Trails of carbon monoxide drifted from every direction. The roughly hewn dirt and rock walls of the mine were supported by thick, rotting beams of timber. Spiders and various other insects scurried along the dirt floor.

"Why did they pick a creepy, dangerous coal mine?" whispered Richard, holding Jeanne-Marie and Jacqueline's hands.

"Probably because it's obviously abandoned and I don't expect anyone to drop by," responded Xerxes Xenon quietly, " and because those villains are burning coal with the carbon dioxide and oxygen prisoners to make more carbon monoxide. What easier place to find coal than a coal mine?"

"They burn the coal because it's hard for the carbon monoxide warriors to capture carbon when it's in its solid state. They can't carry carbon diamonds very easily," whispered Carl Carbon. "But, many carbons live in the coal making it easy for those villians to burn the unsuspecting carbon sleeping in the coal. It's a very dirty trick conspired by the cunning Urban Carbon Monoxide. We must be careful," warned Carl.

"Pssstt... this way to the dungeon," directed Ned Nitrogen.

The frightened elements and children crept along a dark, damp passageway leading further into the mine. In the distance, they could hear the terrified whimper of several small voices. Drawing closer to the feeble cries, the outlines of numerous tiny elements and molecules emerged through the darkness. Soon, the small group could discern a series of thick, black gas-like bars preventing the prisoners from escaping.

"Help us," cried a frail, skinny oxygen atom, barely one tenth the size of Ollie.

"Stand back, we'll free you," said Ned Nitrogen.

"How do you plan on doing that?" asked Xerxes Xenon. "Those bars are thick and we can't risk making another air tunnel. It takes too much energy and time. Plus, it'll make too much noise."

"I'll freeze the bars with a beam of liquid nitrogen. Then all we have to do is break through the bars to rescue the prisoners," suggested Ned Nitrogen.

"And just who is strong enough to break through the frozen barriers. We can't waste time blasting them you idiot," grumbled Xerxes Xenon. "You commoners aren't worth..."

"We can break them," interrupted Richard excitedly. "It'll be like snapping ice sickles."

"Then we'll carry the poor, little elements in our pockets until we get outside," agreed Jacqueline. The three children nervously glanced around the make-shift dungeon.

"Let's do it," said Ollie Oxygen, patting Jeanne-Marie on the head. "Everyone stand back."

"I summon the freezing power of liquid nitrogen," roared Ned Nitrogen, blasting the thick black bars with a watery stream of blinding, reddish-white liquid. "Quickly, get the prisoners. Those bars won't stay frozen for long."

"We got them," yelled Richard, smashing a rock against the frozen bars snapping and crushing the rods of gas. The scrawny oxygen elements and fatigued carbon dioxide molecules struggled to clamber into Jacqueline's hands. Gently sliding the little gases into her pocket, Jacqueline turned to assist Jeanne-Marie and Richard who busily stuffed the coal containing the sleeping carbons into a paper sack.

"There's no escape," cackled a sinister voice, shaking the cave and knocking the children and elements to the roughly hewn floor. "You shall die in the flames of Coal Mine." His taunting, cackling laugh echoed through the cavern sending spine-tingling chills through the terrified band of children and elements.

"He's here," gulped Carl Carbon, springing to his feet. "Look out, behind you."

"By the power of the elements, let there be xenon," roared Xerxes, flashing a blinding greenish beam at the charging carbon monoxide warriors momentarily blinding them.

"Oxygen," yelled Ollie. Streaks of blue shot from his clenched fists smashing into one of the evil henchmen and slicing through another leaving corpse-like blobs of writhing gas.

"Richard, Jacqueline, Jeanne-Marie, run; these small carbon monoxide warriors can't harm you. Don't get near Urban Carbon Monoxide or you won't be able to breathe," warned Xerxes. He and Ned Nitrogen dashed ahead shooting brilliant streams of red and green rays illuminating the tunnel.

"Come on girls, hold my hand and follow me," shouted Richard above the roar of the battle. He began to feel light headed and dizzy. *The carbon monoxide must be getting to me. We've got to get some fresh air*, thought Richard.

The crew of elements and children frantically scrambled down a side tunnel leading away from the giant flames at the end of the mine. Black legions of carbon monoxide oozed and slithered from every tunnel. The group of seven huddled together trapped with no escape. With their backs against the cave wall, the children stared wide-eyed at the advancing legions of carbon monoxide. Frantically attempting to shield themselves, the children collapsed to the rough, jagged floor admist a blinding flash of light.

"It's Arla Argon," cried Xerxes, cheering and diving behind her protective pinkish, oval shield. "Where are Anthony and Catherine?" asked Xerxes Xenon; the rest of the group scrambled to join Xerxes behind Arla's shield.

"They're safe outside. I slipped into the cave before Urban Carbon Monoxide got here," answered Arla Argon. "My shield should hold off those stinky henchmen for a while."

Ollie Oxygen stretched his open palms above his head discharging hundreds of thin blue rays forming an oxygen bubble around the group. The three children gasped for air eager to breathe freely again. Their moment of joy ended abruptly with the hideous Urban Carbon Monoxide slithering into the tunnel.

"You foolish runts," bellowed Urban, choking the tunnel with a black burst of smoke. "You element guardians will help me make an even greater army of carbon monoxide. No one can withstand the power of carbon monoxide," roared Urban, smashing Arla's shield as his wicked warriors fired streaks of black poisonous gas.

"I've been hit," screamed Carl Carbon. Beams of gas slammed him against the rocky wall knocking his small

body to the ground with a horrendous thud. Richard stared in disbelief at the limp body of the little carbon guardian. Slowly raising his head, Richard stood momentarily transfixed in the bone-chilling gaze of Urban Carbon Monoxide. Struggling for air as the carbon monoxide slowly smothered the remaining oxygen in the tunnel, Richard wondered if he was doomed to become like the skeletons explorers and adventurers always seemed to find in those horror movies he had watched. How he wished this was only a movie. Urban Carbon Monoxide's hideous figure slithered closer destroying any chance that this was only a bad movie or dream.

"You'll never take us alive," yelled Xerxes Xenon, aiming his clenched fists at the enormous CO imprinted on Urban Carbon Monoxide's chest. A glorious, icy white light exploded around Urban Carbon Monoxide freezing the walls and floor of the tunnel hurling Urban to the ground shattering him into smaller pieces. "Wow, that's never worked like that before," gasped Xerxes, gazing at his hands.

A shimmering white figure glided into the tunnel revealing a thin beautiful figure, dripping sparkling flakes of ice from long flowing strands of glistening hair. Embroidered upon the front of her long sweeping gown were the words CO2 in glimmering white. Gentle puffs of white smoke rose from the base of her gown.

"You saved us Diana," yelled Arla Argon, cheering ecstatically. A moment ago Richard was sure they would never again see the light of day. Now, a warm river of joy flooded over him where seconds before hopelessness overwhelmed him.

"Thanks Di Carbon Dioxide," chanted the elements.

"It's not over," growled Urban Carbon Monoxide; the last of his oozing black cloud slipped through a crack in the jagged ceiling of the tunnel. "We will meet again! You may have won this battle but I will win the war," threatened Urban in a sinister lethal tone, sending uncontrollable shivers up and down the spines of all those present in the tunnel.

"What about Carl Carbon? Is he going to live?" cried Jeanne-Marie; tears streaked down her face dripping onto the head of her stuffed kangaroo.

"I'm okay," exclaimed Carl Carbon cheerfully. "I was able to transform into a solid before I got shot. Not even Urban Carbon Monoxide is powerful enough to cut through a diamond," said Carl, glittering in the white light cast by Di Carbon Dioxide.

"How did you freeze everything?" asked Richard who like his younger sisters was baffled yet happy to be out of danger.

"I have the power to create dry ice which doesn't melt like an ice cube. This allows me to freeze objects at much colder temperatures. My power can freeze almost anything for hours. When I'm done, the dry ice changes directly into a gas through a magical process called sublimation," replied Di Carbon Dioxide, leading the group out of the coal mine. "I will put out the fire in the back of the mine. Thank you for your helping in the fight against carbon monoxide. Don't forget to warn those humans who may be unknowingly creating deadly amounts of poisonous carbon monoxide," said Di, waving and disappearing into the mine.

"Long live the element guardians," cheered the free prisoners, climbing from the children's pockets.

"Long live the brave human guardians," chanted the elements, waving good-bye to the children.

Back in the dilapidated old shack now full of clean air, the five brothers and sisters slowly removed their element glasses placing them in the tattered gray box. What adventures would their glasses lead them to next? What new elements would they meet? What villains would they encounter? Would they ever completely defeat Urban Carbon Monoxide? It had been a long day. These questions could wait. Turning towards the door, the children slowly exited the cabin and strolled towards their warm, inviting home knowing they accomplished something great.

Episode Three
Sunglasses in School

"Brrrring," echoed the ancient bells throughout the narrow halls of the crowded elementary school. Catherine slid into her desk excitedly chatting with Tiffany. Luckily for her, she sat in the last desk of the row far from the stern gaze of Ms. Birdfoot. Reaching into her backpack, Catherine withdrew her green element glasses and quietly slipped them onto her freckled face. Slouching behind her math book, she mischievously winked at her element friend, Ollie Oxygen, lazily reclining against her history book.

"Any problems today?" whispered Catherine, wishing she was anywhere except for in this classroom.

"Nope," said Ollie, yawning and tucking his cape under his head as if it were a pillow. Folding his arms across the large white O imprinted upon his plump belly, Ollie closed his eyes.

"Miss Catherine," snapped Ms. Birdfoot. "What are you doing back there? Is there something you'd like to share with the class?"

"No ma'am," answered Catherine quickly, jerking her head upwards forgetting she was wearing her element glasses.

"Sunglasses," shouted Ms. Birdfoot, appalled at her student's behavior. "What is the meaning of this young lady? You are in school, not at the beach," scolded the teacher. The other students began to giggle infuriating Ms. Birdfoot further.

"Boy, I wish I was at the beach," muttered Catherine under her breath.

"What was that?" snapped Ms. Birdfoot, snatching a ruler from her desk and marching towards the terrified ten year-old. "Remove those sunglasses at once. We will not have such unacceptable behavior in this classroom."

"I... I'm sorry," stammered Catherine. Ollie Oxygen sprang to his feet and hid behind the bewildered girl's long, tangled red hair. "I ... umm... had to go to the eye doctor. And... umm.. the bright light hurts my eyes especially after the doctor put those drops in them... uhh... to check to see if I need glasses," lied Catherine, trembling in fear.

"Is that so," responded Ms. Birdfoot, not quite believing her student's story. "And just where is your note from the doctor?"

"Ummm... ri... right here," stuttered Catherine, reaching into her notebook; not knowing what to do, but also realizing she had no such note. *Boy, how one lie leads to another and another and another*, thought Catherine, desperately flipping through the pages in her notebook.

At that moment, a small pear-shaped, silvery-white element with a large soft-blue Ca across his chest clambered onto the top of her notebook. Mischievously winking at Catherine, he rapidly jotted a short note on her paper and signed it Dr. Caspar Calcium, certified optometrist. The little element immediately sprang to his feet hooking a tiny tooth-shaped object, with which he had been writing, to the blue chain around his neck. Giving Catherine a thumbs-up, he darted towards Ollie Oxygen.

"What are you staring at?" snapped Ms. Birdfoot, growing more agitated.

"Oh, oh nothing," answered Catherine, grabbing the sheet of paper upon which the element had scribbled. "Here's my note. I found it."

"What's this? I've never heard of this eye doctor and I've definitely never seen a doctor write a note in chalk," said Ms. Birdfoot.

"He... umm... ran out of ink and... umm... could only find a piece of chalk to write with," stammered Catherine on the brink of surrendering and admitting she had been lying. *I'll probably be sent to the principal's office*, thought Catherine, fearing her world was going to end.

"Hmmmm... I don't know about all of this. But, this once I'll let it go. Don't let something like this happen again. Do you understand me?" asked Ms. Birdfoot, folding the note and sticking it in her pocket.

"Yes ma'am," answered Catherine, breathing a sigh of relief, "from now on I'll get my eyes checked after school. You'll never see these sunglasses again. I promise," swore Catherine, joyously watching Ms. Birdfoot march to the front of the room.

"Chalk," whispered Catherine, glaring at the silvery-white element. "Are you trying to get me in trouble?"

"I'm sorry but that's all I had to write with especially since chalk is what I help to make. I'm Caspar Calcium. I'm not only good for your bones and teeth but I also make up a large part of the chalk you use in this classroom," replied Caspar.

Blushing, Catherine realized she was acting unfairly especially since the little element made a sincere effort to get her out of trouble. She realized the element deserved the right to be disappointed in her rude reaction to his kindness.

"Oh, that's why you have that little tooth around your neck," whispered Catherine, covering her mouth with her hand to prevent anyone from noticing she was talking.

"Exactly, it's a piece of chalk," said Caspar Calcium, toying with his necklace.

"Why aren't you blue like Ollie?" asked Catherine, glancing about to assure that no one was staring at her.

"Oh, I'm a metal. I can't fly about as easily as Ollie. In a manner of speaking, I'm stuck to the ground and have to mostly walk. That's why I'm white instead of blue. If I was blue, I might be able to fly like the air elements," answered Caspar, climbing down from Catherine's shoulder and plopping onto her desk.

"Ah, you poor thing. You can't fly," said Catherine, becoming concerned Caspar Calcium would be left behind when the other elements departed.

"Oh, don't worry I can usually connect with oxygen and form a molecule that will allow me to move more quickly. Besides, I like being on the ground since I make up about three and a half percent of the earth's crust. That way, you can find me everywhere even in milk and I get to remain close to the little atoms I protect. I'm the calcium guardian," said Caspar Calcium, performing a handstand on Catherine's desk making her laugh.

"Is something funny Miss Sunglasses?" snapped Ms. Birdfoot, glaring at Catherine. "Since you seem to be having so much fun, maybe you would like to answer the question I just asked Julie."

"Calcium," exclaimed Catherine as Caspar began scribbling in her math book.

"Correct," said the shocked Ms. Birdfoot. "Class, Catherine is correct in stating that calcium helps you to flex your muscles," continued Ms. Birdfoot.

Catherine knew both her and her teacher were amazed a ten year-old should appear familiar with such a scientific fact. Blushing, Catherine grinned as if she knew the answer all along and then sternly glared at Caspar who had quit scribbling and now wrung his hands worried he had done something awful. "Caspar, you can't write in my books. I'll get in trouble," scolded Catherine. "But thanks for doing it. You actually helped me answer the question. That's twice you've saved me. Thanks," whispered Catherine, smiling at Caspar.

"Catherine, who are you talking to?" asked Tiffany, staring at Catherine's desk but not seeing anything unusual.

"Umm... no one," answered Catherine hurriedly. "I was talking to myself."

"Oh... okay," said Tiffany. "What do you want to do on the playground during recess?"

"Let's play chase with the boys. I'm tired of playing house especially since I'm always the baby," answered Catherine. Caspar comically scratched his head and shrugged his shoulders.

"Tiffany and Catherine," yelled an exasperated Ms. Birdfoot. "Is there something you wish to share with the class?"

"No ma'am," answered Catherine, knowing she was in serious trouble this time.

"That does it. I've had all I can take," exclaimed Ms. Birdfoot, reaching for her ruler. "Miss Catherine there will be no recess for you today. Instead you'll write 'I will not talk or wear sunglasses in class' on the chalkboard fifty times," said Ms. Birdfoot, smacking her ruler against the board. "After that, you will clean the erasers. Do you understand me?"

"Yes ma'am," answered Catherine, slumping in her desk.

"Sit up straight young lady," snapped Ms. Birdfoot. "And as for you Miss Tiffany, consider this a warning. One more peep out of you and you will be joining Catherine in here at recess."

"Yes ma'am," said Tiffany, sitting as straight as possible. She wasn't going to miss recess for anything; no matter how strange Catherine acted.

As Ms. Birdfoot turned her attention to the problem she had written upon the board, a black shadow crept past the window.

"Urban Carbon Monoxide," screamed Catherine, recalling the elements' terrible battle with the poisonous villain.

"What?" shouted Ms. Birdfoot. "Have you lost your mind? Young lady you are in..."

"Brrring," rang the bell, announcing lunch and recess. The children sprinted for the door and raced towards the cafeteria.

"Saved by the bell," muttered Catherine, afraid to look at Ms. Birdfoot towering over her desk.

"One more outburst like that and you will win a trip to the principal's office," threatened Ms. Birdfoot, angrily tapping her bony foot on the wooden floor of the classroom. "I'm going to lunch. When I get back, I want to see you finished with your punishment," declared Ms. Birdfoot, stomping out of the classroom.

"That wasn't Urban Carbon Monoxide," giggled Ollie. "That's only a shadow cast by the clouds. We chased Urban far from here. It'll take him a while to regain his strength. I wish we could have found him but he's such a sneaky scoundrel. He managed to escape again. He'll eventually be back; and, we'll be ready for him."

"Uggghhh," whined Catherine. "How am I ever going to write 'I will not talk or wear sunglasses in class' fifty times before Ms. Birdfoot finishes lunch?"

"Don't worry. I've got it all under control," answered Caspar Calcium, hopping to the floor and grabbing the tiny tooth about his neck. Holding the tooth in both hands, Caspar closed his eyes and chanted, "By the power of calcium, let there be chalk." With a sudden flash, a sparkling white powder coated the board revealing the words 'I will not talk or <u>where</u> sunglasses in class' fifty times.

"Wow," exclaimed Catherine. "You..." she began before being startled by Ollie's outburst.

"By the power of the elements, let there be oxygen." A brilliant blue stream of oxygen exploded from Ollie Oxygen's clenched fist blowing the excess chalk from the erasers sitting on the ledge in front of the chalkboard.

"Thanks," said Catherine, sniffling; a tear of joy trickled down her freckled face. Her day finally began to look brighter. "What do we do now?"

"This strawberry jam and peanut butter sandwich looks yummy," said Caspar, digging through Catherine's green colored lunch box.

"Get out of there," ordered Catherine whose stomach growled uncontrollably. "You're always getting in and out of trouble," she said, glaring at the little element who scrambled for cover behind Catherine's backpack.

Grabbing her lunch box and heaving it onto her desk, Catherine contentedly munched on her sandwich. Ollie and Caspar made themselves comfortable in Catherine's sweater and fell asleep. Quickly finishing her sandwich as the door knob to the classroom began to turn, Catherine wiped her mouth with her penguin-decorated shirt sleeve and sat rigidly in her desk. The door creaked open and in stepped Ms. Birdfoot adjusting the glasses resting precariously on the edge of her sharp, pointed nose.

"You misspelled <u>wear</u> fifty times," snapped Ms. Birdfoot, crossing her thin arms.

"Oops," groaned Caspar, slamming his hand against his head.

"Oh, I'm sorry. I'll correct it immediately," said Catherine, glaring at Caspar. The little calcium element shrugged his shoulders and timidly stared at the floor.

"You better believe you will," said Ms. Birdfoot, keenly watching Catherine with hawk-like eyes.

As the little red-haired girl corrected Caspar's mistake, a reddish-yellow blob with sinister yellow eyes plodded past her. Afraid to make another sound, the frightened student rapidly corrected the misspelled word and hurried to her seat.

"What is that?" whispered Catherine, keeping an eye on her teacher. Ms. Birdfoot oblivious to Catherine's con-

Gg Hh Ii Jj Kk Ll
class. I will not talk or where sunglasses in class.
class. I will not talk or where sunglasses in class.
in class. I will not talk or where sunglasses

versation with Caspar made numerous red marks on the test papers at her desk.

"That's the poisonous Litharge," shrieked Caspar Calcium. "We've got to follow him into the hall. Act sick and try to meet us there. You'll definitely be sick if Litharge gets you."

"Lith.. who?" asked Catherine, totally confused yet very frightened.

"Li-th-ar-ge," pronounced Ollie Oxygen. "He's an evil cousin of Urban Carbon Monoxide. Though much smaller in size, he too is deadly," warned Ollie, racing out of the room with Caspar Calcium close on his heels.

Watching her friends slip under the door, Catherine took a deep breath and held it for as long as possible. Exhaling sharply, she began coughing violently. "Oooooohhh," moaned the thin little girl, turning slightly blue from having held her breath for such a long time. "I feel sick."

"Are you okay?" asked Ms. Birdfoot. Catherine cringed, knowing her sick act would be a hard one for her teacher to believe. "Well that's what you get for misbehaving today. I'll give you a pass to the clinic but I'm also going to give you a note to take home to your mother. I have a strong feeling you've been lying and even if you haven't; the other stunts you pulled in class today have been intolerable and inexcusable. We can't risk getting the rest of the class sick though," said the gray-haired teacher, jotting a quick note and handing it to Catherine.

The befreckled girl slowly dragged herself out of the classroom careful not to act too excited about leaving even though she dreaded giving the note to her mother. She would worry about the note later, once this business of Litharge was settled. In the hall, she sprinted to catch Ollie and Caspar. Overjoyed to finally be free of the dreaded classroom, she joined Ollie and Caspar next to the water fountain. With most of the students at recess, the halls were empty.

"We have to wait for another element to get here," said Ollie, breaking the silence. "Being one of the heaviest and oldest metal elements; he's a little slow."

"That's okay," replied Catherine, leaning against the beige colored wall. "I'm glad the morning is finally over. I thought I'd never get out of trouble." As the two elements giggled, Catherine thought *Next time, I won't lie as much and will hopefully not get in as much trouble and will definitely avoid getting this disciplinary note. But, I can't let anyone touch my element glasses, not even Ms. Birdfoot.* Slightly tired from having awakened early in the morning to attend school, the young girl slid down the wall and sat upon the dull white floor. Staring into the distance, she attempted to force the image of the awful Litharge from her mind and wondered what would happen next; once the old, heavy element, Ollie had mentioned, arrived.

Episode Four
Litharge Threatens Art Class

Crouching in the hall after tricking Ms. Birdfoot into thinking her student was sick and needed to go to the clinic, Catherine eagerly awaited the arrival of an old, heavy metal element. Her two element friends, Ollie Oxygen and Caspar Calcium, impatiently paced to and fro as the evil, poisonous Litharge plodded down the hall turning towards the school's art room. Into the hall trudged a bluish-gray element with the letters Pb inscribed upon the front of his cloak, he had a wrinkled face unlike the smooth features of the other elements. Instead of a cape, he wore a long brown cloak that about him covering even his feet. He wielded a small lead pipe which was dwarfed by his unusually large size. Except for being about a half-size larger than the other elements, he possessed no other distinguishing physical features except for the long, bluish-gray beard hanging from his chin.

"Hurry Mr. Plumbum," shouted Caspar Calcium.

"What a strange name," said Catherine, quizzically examining the old element.

"Actually, his name is Lead Plumbum," said Ollie impatiently. "Since he is one of the oldest metals, Mr. Plumbum prefers to go by Plumbum because his name comes from a very old language called Latin. Don't tell him; but in English, Plumbum means lead. Thus, his name is actually Lead Lead. He has forgotten about that over the past four thousand years of his life. He meant to change his first name but never got around to it. Just call him Mr. Plumbum."

"Wow, he's four thousand years-old," exclaimed Catherine who couldn't imagine anything more ancient than her parents' high school pictures. "No wonder he's so old and heavy..."

"Actually, he's much older than four thousand and yes he's quite dense indeed and I don't just mean heavy but also dumb. Please forgive me, that was a bit harsh. Mr. Plumbum isn't dumb; he's actually only slightly forgetful," interjected Caspar Calcium.

"Forgetful," gasped Catherine, hoping the old element wouldn't get lost on his way down the hall.

"I'm afraid he's becoming too old to be an element guardian," said Ollie Oxygen. "At first, forgetting to check on the progress of lead elements wasn't much of a problem; but now, those lead elements have been sitting for too long. The little elements don't know what to do if their guardian doesn't give them new instructions."

"Then what are the lead elements doing?" asked Catherine, wondering what was wrong with lead elements hanging around everywhere.

"The problem with those lead elements is that they've become poisonous. Even worse, lead elements are found in paint, gasoline, and pipes such as the ones leading to this water fountain," said Ollie, peering at the plumbing feeding into the water fountain.

"That's horrible," gasped Catherine. "They don't really mean any harm. They just don't know better. Right?"

"You're right," agreed Caspar, "and people are attempting to solve the problem by removing old lead pipes and paint. They are also removing lead from the gasoline used in cars..."

"The problem is Litharge uses lead to form his poisons," interrupted Caspar Calcium.

"Oh, that's why Litharge has a big yellow PbO; because, Pb stands for lead or ...umm... plumbum as Mr. Plumbum likes to say," said Catherine, disgusted at the thought of the horrid Litharge oozing by her. "I guess that means the O is for oxygen."

"Yep," agreed Caspar, running towards Mr. Lead Plumbum. "You can call that criminal Litharge Lead Monoxide. He's as ruthless as his cousin Urban Carbon Monoxide from the corrupt family of Monoxide."

"Hello Mary," greeted Mr. Lead Plumbum, leaning on his lead staff.

"Her name is Catherine," scolded Caspar Calcium who Catherine noted was frustrated from having to wait for Mr. Plumbum. "Now let's go. Ned Nitrogen and Xerxes Xenon have tracked Litharge Lead Monoxide into the art room and are awaiting our arrival," said Caspar. The group turned the corner and quickly arrived at the door to the art room.

Peering inside the room, Catherine stared in horror. A blinding stream of icy red liquid shot from Ned Nitrogen's clenched fist. The beam of red exploded in front of Litharge Lead Monoxide freezing him in liquid nitrogen. In stunned silence, Catherine watched Litharge shatter the icy liquid nitrogen surrounding him. Ned Nitrogen and Xerxes Xenon quickly slipped under the door narrowly escaping Litharge's reddish-yellow beams of death. Joining the other elements and Catherine in the hall, Xerxes mopped his brow with his hat. "We've got to stop him," declared Xerxes, authoritatively resetting his green hat upon his head.

"I can't go in there," exclaimed Catherine. "There're kids in there. They can't see what's happening. If I go in there and start yelling and talking to you, I'll look like an idiot. They'll think I went crazy. They'll even send me to the doctor."

"You're right," agreed Ned Nitrogen. "You wait here. We need to get Litharge away from the glaze."

"Glaze?" asked Catherine, a little confused.

"Did you miss art class too?" asked Xerxes Xenon. Catherine could sense by the disappointment in his face that he was appalled she wasn't better cultured in the fine arts. "Being an educated noble gas, I will introduce you to pottery. Glaze is used to decorate and waterproof the clay used in making pottery. Simple enough, but if Litharge gets to the glaze, he will combine with it to form lead glaze."

"If that happens, all of the children in that room will be exposed to Litharge's poison," said Ned, sarcastically bowing before Xerxes. "The kids may not only get sick but they could die."

"Stand back," ordered Mr. Lead Plumbum, raising a trembling hand skyward. Pointing his staff at the floor, Mr. Plumbum glared at Litharge. "By the ancient power of the metals, let there be lead," roared Mr. Plumbum in a thunderous voice causing Catherine to tingle with anticipation. She couldn't believe the power surging from the feeble looking Mr. Plumbum. A dazzling bluish-gray stream shot along the floor, under the door, and surrounded the disgusting reddish-yellow blob of Litharge. In a metallic eruption showering the blob in bluish-gray sparks, the lead ring encircling Litharge stretched upwards and spun rapidly in tornado-like fashion until it completely covered Litharge Lead Monoxide in a bluish-gray cage.

"Are you lost Miss Catherine?" snapped Ms. Birdfoot, rounding the corner on her way to speak with Mr. Da Vinci, the art teacher. "Did you forget something in the art room? Do I need to make a phone call to your mother?"

"N... no ma'am," stammered Catherine, knowing she was in for it this time. "I thought I saw flames coming from this room and..."

"Well I hope you did see flames," interrupted Ms. Birdfoot, glaring at Catherine through the spectacles propped upon the end of her nose. "Mr. Da Vinci is going to fire, or rather, bake the children's pottery in the furnace once they put the glaze on their clay cups. Now march yourself to the clinic before you get someone sick," ordered Ms. Birdfoot, pointing a slender, bony finger towards the opposite end of the hall.

"Yes ma'am," said Catherine, pretending to drag herself down the hall as if she were the four thousand plus year-old Mr. Plumbum.

"My that child must really be sick," muttered Ms. Birdfoot, turning and entering the art room.

"This is worse than I thought," said Ned Nitrogen worriedly. "If Litharge contaminates the glaze, those students will be in even greater danger when they fire the pottery."

Making sure Ms. Birdfoot was out of sight, Catherine crouched behind a large, cylindrical trash can in the hall.

"Poo-wee," blurted Caspar Calcium, holding his nose. "What an awful place to have to hide, but at least you're away from Ms. Birdfoot."

"I know," said Catherine, holding her nose and breathing noisily through her mouth. "I'll wait here until Ms. Birdfoot leaves the art room."

"Okay, but quit breathing so hard. You sound like a horse. The whole school is going to hear you," scolded Caspar, disconnecting the tooth from the chain around his neck. "Let's play tic-tac-toe while we wait," suggested Caspar, drawing a four-square grid on the blue trash can.

"Stop that," scolded Catherine. "If I get caught, I'll definitely be in trouble for writing on the garbage can."

"Oops, sorry," said Caspar, shyly rubbing his tooth between his forefinger and thumb. "You sure can't do much around this place."

"Tell me about it," grumbled Catherine, folding her arms across her knees.

The four remaining elements slipped under the art room door and darted towards Litharge Lead Monoxide. As Ollie Oxygen and Ned Nitrogen, who were the faster of the four elements, approached Litharge, a spine-tingling scream froze the elements in their tracks. The bluish-gray cage encasing Litharge Lead Monoxide swelled and stretched. Cringing in terror, the elements dove for cover. A reddish-yellow streak shot through the roof of the cage scattering bluish-gray shards of lead narrowly missing the fleeing elements.

"How dare you toy with me you pathetic atoms. You are no match for the powers of a molecule. I'll crush you," growled Litharge, growing to a height four times the size of the elements.

"It's a trick," warned Mr. Lead Plumbum. "He's only stretched himself. He's no stronger. Lead is stretchable and since he is part lead, he has only formed an illusion by spreading himself thinner. I can do the same trick with my lead staff," said Mr. Plumbum, twirling his staff. With each spin, the ancient element's staff appeared to augment in length.

"Well, if it isn't the wise old Mr. Plumbum. As wise as you have become, you have grown even more feeble in your old age. You are no match for my powers even if you aren't deceived by my tricks," said Litharge Lead Monoxide, his form shifting and wavering. With the elements staring in disbelief, Litharge melted like molten lava and reformed in the shape of an enormous blob with five whip-like tentacles dancing about the yellow PbO glowing on his chest. "You are too late. The glaze is mine. Those children will be mine too," roared Litharge, firing five blood red rays into the glaze causing it to radiate a reddish-yellow. Turning his attention to the elements, Litharge emitted a blood-freezing scream, "Feel the wrath of the all-mighty Litharge." Five more blood red rays exploded into the air.

"Nitrogen," roared Ned, blasting an icy red stream from his fist intercepting Litharge's rays of death, freezing them in mid-air.

"By the noble powers of gas, let there be xenon," yelled Xerxes, firing a blinding green beam exploding before Litharge Lead Monoxide momentarily blinding him.

"By the mystical powers of the ancient metals, let there be lead," roared Mr. Plumbum, holding his staff above his head. Ollie and the other elements darted behind the ancient metal. A sheet of dazzling bluish-gray erupted from Mr. Plumbum's staff forming a metallic wall of lead in front of the foursome. Rays of red continued to whip from Litharge's gruesome tentacles smashing into the wall. The black and white checkered floor of the art room disappeared beneath the oozing blob of Litharge. Hues of flashing red, green, and blue illuminated the elementary student's illustrations decorating the beige wall of the art room.

"This shield won't hold much longer," shouted Ned Nitrogen, firing an icy red blast at Litharge freezing one of his gnarled tentacles.

Back in the hall, Caspar Calcium peeked around the trash can. "There goes Ms. Birdfoot. Follow me. We have to get to the other elements. They may be in grave danger."

"Don't say that; do you think they're okay?" asked Catherine, concerned her best friend, Ollie Oxygen, might be hurt.

"I don't know," replied Caspar, racing down the hall with Catherine behind him. "But with Mr. Plumbum in there, they might be safe. Even though Mr. Plumbum is old and forgetful, it's extremely hard for someone to fool him. Besides, his powers are stronger than most of the other elements' powers even though he's grown weaker with age."

Arriving at the art room door, the little red-haired girl stood on the tip of her toes and peered through the window in horror. Brilliant red, blue, and green streaks exploded through the air. At the opposite end of the room, the children and Mr. Da Vinci, unaware of the destructive battle being waged in that very room, prepared to begin adding the poisonous lead glaze to their clay cups. With tears in her eyes, Catherine watched the lead wall in front

of the elements explode in an eruption of reddish-yellow slamming Ned Nitrogen to the floor. Taunting the elements, Litharge Lead Monoxide erupted in a burst of chilling, haunting laughter. A flood of reddish-yellow rays whipped from his tentacles exploding about the fleeing elements whose return fire seemed to have no apparent effect. As the elements struggled to slip under the art room door, a blast slammed into Xerxes Xenon knocking him into the wall. Xerxes lifeless body landed with a thud and lay motionless. His green hat floated to the floor. Litharge Lead Monoxide slithered towards the limp bodies of the two elements.

"We have to save them," cried Catherine, staring in terror at the wickedly twisted face of Litharge whose two beady, yellow eyes flickered like a pair of fiery embers.

"Catherine, grab the container of glaze and warn Mr. Da Vinci of its danger," ordered Mr. Plumbum, pointing his staff towards Catherine. A stream of bluish-gray shot from the old element's staff forming a pair of metallic gloves around the stunned ten year-old's hands. "These lead gloves will protect you from the radiation and poison leaking from the glowing glaze. Wait until we enter the room before you grab the glaze."

"We'll attempt to create our own lead monoxide to neutralize Litharge," said Ollie Oxygen. "At the very least, we'll divert his attention long enough for you to snag the glaze."

"I thought you couldn't form evil molecules," gasped Catherine, afraid of the potential damage two Litharge's could create.

"We can't," assured Mr. Lead Plumbum. "But lead monoxide is capable of creating good such as in helping to make rubber and lead glass. This Litharge has chosen to convert all lead monoxide to become part of his sinister army."

"By creating a good, positive lead monoxide, we should be able to freeze the negative, evil Litharge neutralizing him long enough for us to transport him to Molecule Prison," said Ollie Oxygen.

"We'll tell you more about Molecule Prison at another time," said Mr. Lead Plumbum, waddling under the door.

"You foolish, feeble old element," growled Litharge Lead Monoxide. "Meet your doom. You will join your puny friends," screamed Litharge, aiming his tentacles at Mr. Plumbum.

"You're wrong. Your time has come Litharge," declared Mr. Lead Plumbum, raising his staff above his head. "By the ancient secrets of metal, let there be lead," yelled Mr. Plumbum, shooting a blazing stream of bluish-gray at the oozing Litharge who bellowed with hideous laughter.

"By the power of oxygen, let there be lead monoxide," shouted Ollie Oxygen, firing a brilliant blue beam into the bluish-gray stream of Mr. Plumbum.

"What?" screamed Litharge, desperately unleashing a barrage of streaks at the twisting beams of Ollie and Mr. Plumbum. The two elements' beams continued spinning more and more rapidly exploding into a reddish-yellow blob violently slamming into Litharge. "Noooo..." shrieked Litharge, frantically waving his tentacles. The blob slowly swallowed Litharge forming a solid mass which collapsed motionless in the middle of the checkered floor.

"Run Catherine. Grab the glaze container," exclaimed Caspar Calcium. Mr. Da Vinci slowly reached for the glaze.

Dashing into the art room, Catherine made a frantic dive at the table on which rested the poisonous container of glaze. Crashing into the table and scattering its contents across the room, Catherine desperately reached for the glaze plunging towards the floor. Mr. Da Vinci and his students stared with gaping mouths, in stunned silence, watching the container plummet ever closer towards the ground.

"Got it," exclaimed Catherine, snagging the container seconds before it smashed onto the floor.

"You're going to get it all right," hollered Mr. Da Vinci. "What's the meaning of this? Explain yourself? Young girl, have you gone mad?"

"Uhh... no sir," gasped Catherine, gripping the container firmly. "I believe this glaze contains poisonous amounts of lead monoxide."

"What?" exclaimed Mr. Da Vinci, stroking the thin goatee concealing his chin.

"There's too much poisonous lead in here. It'll make everybody sick and could even kill them," responded Catherine, afraid to move. The remaining elements watched helplessly.

"Well Miss Scientist, I happen to have an instrument that will tell me how much lead is in that glaze and we'll see if your accusation is true," said the startled Mr. Da Vinci. Catherine sensed this was an awkward situation for both her and Mr. Da Vinci, who wasn't quite sure how to react. Grabbing his lab equipment and slipping on a pair of lead lined rubber gloves in case this freckled child was right, Mr. Da Vinci waved a metallic wand over the glaze forcing a loud series of electronic beeps to sound from the instrument in his hand. "You're right. This glaze is contaminated," said the amazed Mr. Da Vinci, grabbing the container and placing it in a large rubber canister marked with the words Hazardous Waste. "I don't know how you knew that and I really don't want to know. Maybe it had something to do with those funny looking sunglasses you're wearing."

"Maybe," replied Catherine, turning towards where her two element friends rested silently upon the floor.

"Why don't you sit here until you feel better," said Mr. Da Vinci, gently patting Catherine on the shoulder. "You can return to class whenever you feel better. By the way, nice gloves." The puzzled Mr. Da Vinci removed his lead-lined gloves and turned his attention to his students.

Catherine dejectedly slid to her knees and stared at Xerxes and Ned. Tears trickled down her cheeks. Xerxes might have been slightly pompous but she had grown accustomed to his uppity mannerisms and had even developed a soft spot in her heart for him. Gently lifting Xerxes' small hat from the cold, hard floor, Catherine laid it neatly beside his lifeless, plump body. Ollie Oxygen and Mr. Lead Plumbum somberly bowed their heads. A hush fell over the group as Mr. Da Vinci, unaware of the tragedy that had befallen the element guardians, continued lecturing to his class. Startling everyone, Caspar Calcium grabbed the tooth about his neck and chanted, "By the healing and strengthening power of calcium, may these elements become as strong as bones and as lively as firm muscles." A strange sparkling white powder drifted from Caspar's chain settling over the two motionless bodies.

As the group watched in anticipation, the two elements trembled slightly and suddenly sprang upwards fully revived.

"Where's my hat?" grumbled Xerxes Xenon, quickly scanning the floor. "A noble gas is never without his hat."

"We almost die and all you worry about is your hat," exclaimed Ned Nitrogen, scooping Xerxes' hat off the floor and dashing towards the door.

"Come back here you rotten scoundrel. You common elements have no respect," yelled Xerxes Xenon, chasing after Ned.

"There they go again," giggled Ollie Oxygen, happy to see his two friends return to their normal antics.

"I never get any thanks," muttered Calcium Caspar, shyly hanging his head.

"Don't fret young one. You did fine. You all did exceptionally well. You have made an old element proud," said Mr. Lead Plumbum. "I will deliver this evil Litharge to the authorities at Molecule Prison," said Mr. Plumbum, waving good-bye to the group.

Wiping tears from her eyes, Catherine stood and sauntered towards the art room door. Maybe by saving the class from the poisonous lead, she'd be forgiven for the lying she did earlier. Catherine gently patted her pocket containing the note from her teacher; there were many things worse than being punished for bad behavior. Removing her sun glasses and placing them carefully in her pocket, Catherine hoped there would be no more adventures, at least for a little while.

Episode Five
Terror on Rocky Ridge

"Tent," yelled Richard, checking a list of items needed for the two brothers' weekend camp out.

"Got it," answered Anthony, securing the tent to his large backpack.

"Well, that should do it. I think we have everything," said Richard, carefully folding the list entitled weekend camp out necessities and tucking it in his camouflage-colored coat pocket.

"Should we..." began Anthony, dusting off the tattered gray box with the word elements scrawled across the top of the oaken container.

"I don't know," replied Richard.

"I don't want to have to see that evil molecule again," continued Anthony, recalling their gruesome battle with the hideous Urban Carbon Monoxide.

"What the heck. Let's do it. Maybe the elements can help us and besides they've supposedly chased Urban Carbon Monoxide far from here," said Richard, opening the box and removing a pair of oddly decorated red sun glasses.

"Okay. I'll wear my element glasses too," agreed Anthony, reluctantly slipping on his blue pair.

"Hey," greeted Ned Nitrogen, scratching the enormous cyan N imprinted on his belly. "Where do you plan on camping for the weekend?"

"Up near Rocky Ridge," answered Richard, heaving his backpack onto his shoulders and cinching the straps. "But, not too close to the abandoned coal mine; that place gives me the creeps."

"Yeah," agreed Anthony, following Richard out of the shack and into the woods.

After spending an exhausting morning setting up camp, the two boys prepared to light a carefully arranged pile of logs, branches, and tinder with Ollie Oxygen and Ned Nitrogen watching in amusement. Opening the match box, Anthony gasped in astonishment as out plopped a discontent looking brownish-red element with a large white P on his belly. Glaring at the brown haired thirteen year-old, the walnut shaped element dropped to the forest floor pulling his black cape about him. Sulking around the camp ground, the disgruntled element quit pacing long enough to flop against the wood heap soon to become a roaring camp fire.

"Oh no, not him," groaned Ned Nitrogen, staring at the melancholy new arrival.

"Quickly, light the fire," yelled Ollie Oxygen, floating down from a maple leaf in which he had been leisurely reclining. "That's Pete Phosphorous pronounced *FAHS fuhr uhs*. He's bad news. That character's been in and out of Molecule Prison over a dozen times."

"I thought Molecule Prison was only for wicked molecules. He's only an element," said Anthony, never having met a bad element guardian.

"That's true," said Ollie Oxygen, rubbing his bald head. It seemed to Anthony that Ollie was not quite sure what to do with Pete Phosphorous. "But, Molecule Prison also holds the few element guardians who have turned to the path of evil."

"Who is going to protect the phosphorous atoms if he's in prison?" asked Richard, running his fingers through his tussled red hair.

"Unfortunately, Pete Phosphorous is the chosen guardian of phosphorous. We element guardians have no control over choosing who becomes a guardian. That decision is left to the Great Ones. But, that's another story," said Ollie Oxygen, disappointedly shaking his head.

"It's a shame Pete Phosphorous is a guardian because phosphorous plays such an important role in the growth of plants and animals. In fact, phosphorous is a significant part of a powerful compound, adenosine triphosphate, which supplies plants and animals with energy," interjected Ned Nitrogen.

"Even though he looks grumpy and gloomy, he doesn't seem to be causing any trouble," observed Anthony, preparing to strike a match to light the camp fire.

"Hurry. Start the fire," urged Ollie Oxygen, frantically waving his arms. "If Pete Phosphorous cools down too much, he becomes cold and turns into poisonous white phosphorous."

"White phosphorous?" asked Anthony, quickly igniting the kerosene drenched wood forcing Pete to spring to his feet.

"Yes, Pete will turn white if he becomes cold enough. As long as he remains as red phosphorous, he is no threat to anyone. In fact, he even helps to make the tips of those matches you're holding. But, beware if he becomes white phosphorous," warned Ned Nitrogen, pushing Pete towards the fire to keep him warm.

"As white phosphorous, he's not only poisonous but will also burst into flames. At least he can't hide from you. When he turns white he becomes phosphorescent," said Ollie, blowing on the flames to help them grow larger.

"Phosphor... what?" asked Anthony, slightly confused.

"Phosphorescent," replied Ned Nitrogen. "It means the white phosphorous will glow in the dark."

Blushing uncontrollably, Anthony knew the little element was ashamed someone Anthony's age did not know the meaning of such a word. "Oh," said Anthony meekly. "I remember now. Why don't you keep him in prison?"

"Well, someone must protect the phosphorous elements and he's the only one that knows enough about the secrets of phosphorous to do it. There is another reason why he was in prison though," answered Ollie Oxygen, secretively glancing towards Ned Nitrogen.

"What's that?" asked Richard. Anthony began to grow concerned that their peaceful weekend might be in jeopardy.

"There's no reason to worry you with it," answered Ned Nitrogen, glaring at Pete Phosphorous attempting to sneak away from camp.

"What is it? We want to know. Tell us," insisted Anthony, not wanting to be excluded from a secret.

"In time, you may know. Now is not the time. It will not help you to know," cautioned Ollie Oxygen, helping Ned drag Pete back to the fire.

"Tell the kid," grumbled Pete, flashing a wicked smile. "There will be no sleep for them tonight. They should be very afraid. It would be wise if they knew about..."

"Say another word and I'll blast you," threatened Ned Nitrogen, shaking his clenched fist at the reddish-brown element.

"Oh please do blast me with one of your freezing liquid nitrogen rays," mocked Pete Phosphorous. Anthony trembled fearing the freezing temperatures of Ned's ray would lower Pete's temperature enough to transform him into white phosphorous. Anthony did not want to be involved in another confrontation with an evil element or molecule. The sickening image of Urban Carbon Monoxide was still too vivid a memory for him.

"That's enough," roared Xerxes Xenon, picking his way through the leaves of the trees and joining the other elements.

"Well if it isn't his royal highness," ridiculed Pete Phosphorous, bowing before Xerxes who boiled with rage.

"May the powers of xenon teach you some respect," roared Xerxes Xenon, firing a brilliant green beam slamming Pete Phosphorous to the forest floor, leaving him blind.

"You'll pay for this, you overstuffed uppity wind-bag. Phosphorous," screamed Pete Phosphorous, wildly tossing circular bombs magically emerging from the palm of his hands. As the elements dashed for cover, the reddish-brown bombs exploded in brilliant sparks of red, orange, and blue causing sudden bursts of flame and smoke.

"Stop," yelled Ollie Oxygen. "Pete, you're wasting your energy. You can't see. You're not going to be able to hit anyone. Xerxes don't even think about firing another blast," declared Ollie, winking at Xerxes Xenon before continuing. "We all must cooperate regardless of our dif-

ferences. We're guardians. We're here to protect the elements not to destroy one another."

Collapsing in a heap, Pete Phosphorous sullenly tossed pebbles into the distance. The final rays of the sun flickered below the horizon yielding to the darkness of night, shrouding the camp site. The trees began to assume eerie shapes forcing Richard and Anthony to huddle closer to the warmth of the fire.

"Hey guys. What's up," greeted a cute little element appearing slightly smaller than the other elements. There was a large H across the front of her almond shaped body. She wore a simple white cape that draped loosely about her frame. There was nothing out of the ordinary about her.

"Hi Holly," exclaimed Ned Nitrogen who Anthony noticed seemed to be rather attracted to this light, little element. "We were attempting to enjoy a quiet weekend with nature when the bothersome Pete Phosphorous decided to spoil everything."

"Everything is under control though," said Ollie, glaring at Pete who was beginning to regain his sight. "Have you met the boys?"

"I don't believe I have. No, wait a minute, I did meet them. I believe it was the day you defeated that sinister Urban Carbon Monoxide," said Holly, waving at the two boys. Anthony smiled weakly wishing he had left his element glasses at the shack. He and his brother were in no mood to mess with Pete Phosphorous or to become entangled in another battle with some monstrous molecular villain.

"Well let me refresh their memories," said Ned Nitrogen, grabbing Holly's hand and pulling her toward

Richard and Anthony. "This is Holly Hydrogen. She may be one of the lightest and simplest elements but she makes up a large chunk of the sun and stars. She even helps in creating the fuel used by the space shuttle."

"Thank you," said Holly Hydrogen, blushing. Apparently flattered by Ned's introduction, Holly tugged timidly at the end of her cape.

"Nice to meet you," sounded Anthony and Richard in unison, once again gathering around the camp fire.

The moon glowed brightly through the trees illuminating the camp ground. The two boys lied awake in their sleeping bags unable to doze off after hearing Pete Phosphorous' hauntingly mysterious warning. Snoring loudly, the elements did not seem to share the boy's worries. It seemed as though nothing could wake the guardians from their deep slumber.

"What was that?" asked Anthony, hearing a distant twig snap.

"I don't know," answered Richard, sitting rigidly in his sleeping bag.

"This place is spooky. Let's go home. We can come back in the morning and get our stuff," pleaded Anthony who would have left minutes ago, but he didn't dare venture alone through the woods in the middle of the night. Studying his brother's tense expression, Anthony sensed Richard thought it sounded like a good idea too. He only wished Richard would quit wasting time contemplating leaving the warmth and security of his sleeping bag. If they abandoned camp now, they could be in their warm, safe beds before the last embers of the fire fizzled and grew cold.

"Aaaaaah," screamed Anthony in terror. A large shadow crept across the camp ground, drawing attention to an enormous, dark figure rumbling in front of the smoldering coals that once were a roaring camp fire. A large PO4 glinted in the moon light casting an eerie aura about the dark shadow.

"What?" exclaimed Holly Hydrogen, awakening abruptly, startling the rest of the elements. That is all except for Xerxes Xenon who continued to snore loudly.

"It's Dert Phosphate (*FAHS fayt*)," shouted Ned Nitrogen, shaking Xerxes Xenon in a desperate attempt to awaken him.

"Dert Phosphate," exclaimed Richard. Anthony frantically scrambled from his sleeping bag wishing he had left when they still had the chance.

"Yes, his first name describes the dirt he has become," said Ollie Oxygen, rushing towards the dark figure. "He was once used in making detergents for washing clothes but he soon began to pollute the water and was banned by most cities and states in the United States."

"That only made him angrier and caused him to begin trying to convert Pete Phosphorous to his evil ways," said Ned Nitrogen, finally shaking Xerxes Xenon from his slumber.

"Who dares to wake a noble gas from his royal sleep," growled Xerxes Xenon, rolling over in the soft pile of leaves he had converted into a bed.

"Phosphate is here," exclaimed Ned Nitrogen irritably.

"So what, phosphate is good for the growth of plants and animals. Offer him a cup of hot chocolate and leave me alone," groaned Xerxes Xenon, covering his head with his small cape.

"Not that phosphate," exclaimed Ned, slamming his hand against his forehead. "Dert Phosphate."

"Dert Phosphate," yelled Xerxes Xenon, jumping to his feet. "I thought that scoundrel was in Molecule Prison."

"He escaped with the help of Pete Phosphorous when Pete transformed into white phosphorous," said Ned, dragging Xerxes Xenon in the direction of the hideous figure.

"I should have blasted Pete again. That would have put an end to him permanently," grumbled Xerxes, glaring at Pete Phosphorous who appeared transfixed by the large PO4 radiating from the dark shadow.

"Oh no," moaned Anthony. "That little four on his chest must mean he has four oxygen's connected to his phosphorous. How are we going to destroy him when he's as powerful as four oxygens not to mention the one phosphorous?"

"Hello again Pete," sounded an eerie growl, vibrating from the murky shadows of the lurking figure. "I have come for you. These puny elements can never give you the power I posses. They are worthless. Follow me. Together we'll destroy the elements and free our friends from Molecule Prison."

"Don't listen to him," yelled Holly Hydrogen, attempting to snap Pete Phosphorous from his trance.

"By the royal power of the noble gases, I summon xenon," roared Xerxes, firing a brilliant green blast illuminating the camp and the horribly twisted figure of Dert Phosphate.

"Nitrogen," yelled Ned, blasting Dert Phosphate with an icy liquid stream of red. The blast from Ned glanced off the dark cape of Dert Phosphate slamming into Pete Phosphorous.

"Noooo..." screamed Ned Nitrogen, watching Pete Phosphorous' body flicker reddish-brown for a moment before flashing bleach white. Erupting in flames, Pete glowed brightly in the night air as he began casting poisonous smoldering balls of fire at the elements. Pete's fire balls narrowly missed the element guardians but ignited the dry leaves covering the forest floor.

"They're going to start a forest fire," yelled Anthony, frantically waving his arms. He and Richard grabbed their canteens, dousing the flames before they could spread.

"Water," exclaimed Ollie Oxygen. "That's exactly what we need to stop Pete Phosphorous."

"We don't have anymore," said Anthony, nimbly avoiding the fire balls flaring towards him. "We used it to put out the fire."

"Nitrogen," roared Ned, blasting an icy red liquid from his clenched fist freezing Pete's balls of flame in mid air. "I can't keep this up forever. Think of something, quickly."

"I'm becoming bored watching your pathetic attempts," roared Dert Phosphate, spreading his cape open revealing his massive form. Shrouded in a smoky veil, Dert Phosphate advanced towards the retreating group of elements. "Feel the fury of all the demons of phosphate," shrieked Dert, releasing an army of impish snake-like creatures which slithered from beneath his cloak, each spitting glowing, greenish darts of poison. Anthony stood frozen in fear. Wondering whether he should flee into the dark twisted forest or take his chances with Dert Phosphate; Anthony could only wish he had left his element glasses in the tattered gray box.

"Xenon," roared Xerxes, firing a dazzling green ray, momentarily blinding Pete Phosphorous and the devilish serpents but having no effect upon the diabolical Dert Phosphate.

"We're doomed," exclaimed Anthony, dropping his canteen and fleeing after Richard who desperately sought shelter in the security of the wooded thicket. Anthony did not dare wander out of sight of the camp; but, if the elements couldn't stop Dert, how was he supposed to destroy the sinister molecule?

"You haven't won yet, you monster. How quickly you forget about your one weakness," yelled Holly Hydrogen, raising both arms skyward and pointing her fingers at Dert Phosphate. "By the awesome power of the sun and stars, I summon hydrogen," exclaimed Holly, firing shimmering spirals of spectacular blue completely encircling Dert.

"Nooooooo," shrieked Dert Phosphate as he and his snake-like henchmen dissolved amidst a shower of green and red erupting from Ned and Xerxes.

"Holly, aim at Pete Phosphorous," ordered Ollie Oxygen. Holly fired her spectacular spirals of light at Pete slamming him to the ground.

"Ha, you can't stop me with hydrogen spirals," boasted Pete, jumping to his feet and unleashing another round of fire balls.

"No, but we can with water," declared Ollie Oxygen, pointing a clenched fist at Pete Phosphorous. "By the power of the elements, let there by oxygen," shouted Ollie, blasting a glittering blue beam into Holly's double spirals. Anthony stared in awe gasping at the beauty of Holly's spirals which were easily twice the size of Ollie's beam. The two beams swirled together erupting into a tidal wave of water, H2O, completely drenching Pete Phosphorous who fizzled for a moment before collapsing silently in a muddy puddle.

"As long as we keep him in the water, Pete Phosphorous should cause no more trouble," said Ollie, joyously hugging Holly. "He's only hazardous when he's out of water. In the morning, the sunlight should create enough heat to convert him to his reddish-brown form. Then, we can safely escort him to Molecule Prison where he'll spend another two years making baking soda."

"What about Dert Phosphate?" asked Richard, staring at the oozing greenish glop sinking into the ground.

"Oh him," said Holly Hydrogen, giggling bashfully. "He is nothing more than phosphate fertilizer. When phosphate becomes connected with enough hydrogen, it turns into fertilizer. All I did was make sure Dert Phosphate received a good blast of hydrogen. That's Dert's only weakness."

"I told you she was powerful even though she's petite and delicate," said Ned Nitrogen, proudly hugging Holly.

"Thanks. I was glad I could do something to help," squeaked Holly Hydrogen. Waving good-bye, she darted into the woods.

"Bye Holly," shouted the elements. Ned Nitorgen and Xerxes Xenon raced to see who could find the softest bed of leaves.

"Wow, that was exciting. I'm glad I decided to stay. This has turned into a great camp out," blurted Anthony excitedly. The elements rolled their eyes knowing how lucky they were to still be alive.

"Boy, look at the time," exclaimed Richard, unzipping his sleeping bag. Slowly, the two boys removed their element glasses and climbed into their warm bags. Lying in the darkness, both boys found it difficult to sleep wondering what adventures they would encounter the next time they wore their element glasses.

Episode Six
The Sultan of Sulfur Dioxide

"Jeanne-Marie, wake up. It's Saturday," exclaimed Jacqueline, eagerly bouncing from her bed even though it was only six-thirty in the morning.

"Cartoons," squealed Jeanne-Marie, grabbing her stuffed kangaroo and racing after Jacqueline.

"I'll get the sweet cereal," said Jacqueline, grabbing a box of her favorite sugar-coated flakes from the pantry. The disturbance woke the girls' parents who rolled over and attempted to return to sleep wondering why the two girls couldn't manage to spring from bed on school mornings.

"Let's watch The Adventures of Alex the Catfish," suggested Jeanne-Marie, snatching the remote control and flipping on the television set. The theme song for the acquatic adventure blared from the little, black television resting on a shelf overlooking the kitchen. Pouring two bowls full of cereal, the girls plopped into the stiff wooden chairs surrounding the rectangular kitchen table.

"I love Saturdays. No school," mumbled Jacqueline, stuffing her mouth to capacity with the sugar-coated chocolate flakes.

"Let's wear our element glasses," said Jeanne-Marie, already slipping on her pink colored, strangely-decorated glasses. Not wanting to be excluded from any possible adventures, Jacqueline quickly grabbed her purple glasses.

"Good morning," greeted a plump little fellow, fiddling with a funny green hat upon his head.

"It's Xerxes Xenon," squealed Jeanne-Marie. "Do you like cartoons too?"

"Of course, all elements like cartoons. Too bad they aren't real like us," said Xerxes Xenon, majestically bowing before the two girls causing them to giggle.

"Hi," greeted a silvery-white element with a soft-blue Ca imprinted upon his tummy.

"It's Caspar Calcium," announced Jacqueline excitedly. "Have you come to watch cartoons too?"

"Oh yes, I love cartoons. Watch, I can draw Alex the Catfish," said Caspar Calcium, removing the little tooth from around his neck and attempting to sketch an outline of the catfish upon the wall.

"Oh no, don't write on the wall. Mommy will get mad," said Jacqueline, hurriedly wiping away Caspar's chalk outline.

"Woops, sorry," mumbled Caspar Calcium, timidly shrugging his shoulders.

As the seven year-old, strawberry blond glanced at the television, a silver element wearing a rainbow colored cape drifted from the screen. Yawning as if he had been jolted from a deep slumber, the honeydew melon-size critter scratched the large rainbow-colored Eu on his stomach.

"Good morning Eugene Europium," greeted Xerxes Xenon. "It's about time you woke up. It's almost seven o' clock. We can't waste any of our Saturday sleeping. We save that for school days ... errr ... I mean ... cool days."

"That may work for you. But if you were awake as late at night as I am, you wouldn't be quite as eager to climb out of bed in the morning," said Eugene Europium, sluggishly stretching his arms above his head.

"Why don't ya go to bed earlier?" asked Jeanne-Marie. Jacqueline nodded in agreement, wondering why anyone would want to be awake after eight o' clock at night.

"Oh, I'm the guardian of the europium elements used in making color television screens. Anytime someone turns on the television, I have to go to work. I don't get much sleep especially when everyone leaves there television on all day and night," groaned Eugene Europium irritably. Jacqueline sadly realized people's bad television habits prevented the little element from getting his proper rest. She wondered what other bad things happened from people watching too much television.

"I'm sorry," apologized Jacqueline, concerned the little element would never get any sleep. "We can turn off the TV if it'll make you feel better."

"Don't worry about it. I don't mind watching Saturday morning cartoons. In fact, I think I'll watch this episode of The Adventures of Alex the Catfish. It's a good one," said Eugene Europium, dragging himself exhaustibly to Jeanne-Marie's stuffed kangaroo which appeared like it might make a comfortable bed.

"Europium is a funny sounding name. It sounds like the name of a country," pondered Jacqueline, showing a desire for knowledge through her inquisitive nature.

"Actually, the French scientist, Eugene Demarcay, who first discovered me, named me in honor of Europe," answered Eugene Europium, making himself comfortable in the pouch of Jeanne-Marie's kangaroo.

"Poo-wee, what's that smell?" asked Jeanne-Marie, pinching her nose.

"Yuck, that smells awful. Did somebody forget to take a bath?" asked Jacqueline, suddenly losing her appetite.

"What? Young lady, we nobles never go without a proper cleaning. Our hygiene is immaculate," said Xerxes Xenon. Jacqueline quickly noted Xerxes was offended anyone would insinuate he was malodorous.

"I didn't say you. I said somebody," replied Jacqueline, not in the mood to hear Xerxes Xenon's noble claims especially when she could hardly breathe.

"Oh, yes, that you did. Please accept my apology. I jumped to conclusions too swiftly," replied Xerxes, attempting to hide himself with his cape which was far too short to cover his immense figure.

"You're forgiven," said Jacqueline who was more interested in eliminating the awful smell than in receiving Xerxes' apologies. "That smell's coming from the window."

"The oil refineries must be polluting the air again," said Xerxes.

"It's worse than that," said Caspar Calcium, nervously tugging at the tooth hanging from his neck. "The oil refineries' pollution has summoned the wicked Sultan of Sulfur Dioxide. He must be gathering his armies for another acid rain attack."

"Acid rain," exclaimed Jacqueline, having learned in school the damage acid rain can cause to buildings, crops, and forests.

"As long as those oil refineries continue to release large amounts of sulfur dioxide, the Sultan of Sulfur Dioxide will have plenty of ammunition for his armies," warned Caspar Calcium.

"Where is he?" asked Jacqueline.

"I'm not sure because he has no color making him invisible," answered Xerxes Xenon. "Oh, never mind. I forgot you had your element glasses. In that case, you'll be able to see him although I'm not sure you'll want to see him. Even though he is the brother of Di Carbon Dioxide, he definitely doesn't possess her beauty nor her kindness."

"He's coming," yelled Ollie Oxygen, slipping under the kitchen window and picking his way through the numerous flowers decorating the window ledge. "Someone wake Eugene Europium. We're going to need his help," said Ollie, pointing towards Eugene Europium who peacefully slept, curled up in Jeanne-Marie's kangaroo.

"Look out," screamed Caspar Calcium. A yellow blast streaked through the window. An enormous, billowing mass of yellow smoke-like particles permeated the room. The mass of yellow shifted and wavered until a horrid form emerged. Clothed in majestic robes adorned with a large SO_2, the figure stepped from the cloud and glared at the group. His eyes flickered like two tiny flames and a wispy, thin goatee hung from his chin. Clenching a golden sceptre in one hand, the Sultan curled his black, claw-like fingers into a tight fist.

"By the noble power of the elements, I summon Xenon," roared Xerxes, firing a brilliant green streak that flashed before the Sultan of Sulfur Dioxide.

"Eugene Europium, wake up," yelled Caspar Calcium, tugging at Eugene's brightly colored cape.

"Who wants to watch television now?" grumbled Eugene, barely opening one eye.

"Forget about the television. The Sultan of Sulfur Dioxide is here," screamed Caspar, cringing in fear from the Sultan's chilling laughter.

"Where?" asked Eugene, jumping to his feet. "He'll destroy everything."

"How right you are," hissed the Sultan of Sulfur Dioxide. His forked tongue ominously flickered at the elements. "I will not again be fooled by your rainbow, Eugene. During our previous encounter, you may have tricked me into thinking the sun was weakening my acid rain clouds, but I will not be deceived as easily this time. You are worthless to me. I will crush you."

Boiling with rage at the Sultan's insult, Eugene Europium raised his hands skyward, "By the colors of the rainbow, I summon Europium." A rainbow colored boomerang appeared in each of Eugene's hands. With a great heave, Eugene Europium flung the two boomerangs at the Sultan of Sulfur Dioxide flooding him in a rainbow-like shroud of light. "That should temporarily confuse him. He won't be able to see anything because there are too many colors whirling around him. We have to get out of the house. Quickly, run for the backyard," shouted Eugene Europium, fleeing down the narrow hallway towards the back door almost crashing into a strangely dressed element.

"Hola, amigos," greeted a shiny violet-black element in Spanish; wearing a huge sombrero. "¿Que pasa?"

"What's up? My friend, I'll tell you what's up. The Sultan of Sulfur Dioxide is up," exclaimed Xerxes Xenon, racing past the foreign element with the large I upon his belly. "You should have stayed in Chile where you could have kept playing with those little iodine elements living

84

in your kelp seaweed," said Xerxes, turning and desperately firing another blast at the Sultan.

"Don't stand there Io Iodine. Run, or we'll never again play tic-tac-toe," yelled Caspar Calcium, tightly clutching his chalk tooth and dashing to join the others.

"Yikes," exclaimed Io Iodine. In bewilderment, the motley crew of elements and children froze, gawking at Io who, instead of fleeing, marched towards the Sultan of Sulfur Dioxide.

"He must be sea sick from his long journey or maybe his sombrero is blocking his vision. He's going the wrong way," shouted Xerxes.

"He'll never survive a blast from the wicked eyes of the Sultan. It'll shred him into subatomic particles," exclaimed Ollie Oxygen.

As the group of elements and the two girls stared in horror, Io Iodine chanted a few verses of an ancient hymn which no one in the room could quite comprehend. Immediately, there was a bright reddish flash and a mirror-image of Io Iodine materialized. The two identical iodines swirled into one causing an eruption. When the sparks settled, a purple Io Iodine adorned with a large I_2 radiating from his chest shimmered with an iridescent hue. Levitating into the air, Io grew to twice his original size.

"Wow," shrieked Jeanne-Marie, hugging her kangaroo. "How'd he do that?"

"Io is from the mystical family of the Halogens. They posses the power to create a magical diatomic molecule by connecting to another identical element forming, in this case, a large iodine gas," stated Xerxes. Glancing at Xerxes, Jacqueline could detect a hint of jealousy. She thought *maybe he wished he could do the same especial-*

ly since he was supposed to be a high and mighty noble gas. "A few other elements such as Ollie Oxygen can do the same. If you will note, I am already a gas without having to go through such a ridiculous spectacle," said Xerxes Xenon, puffing out his chest and holding his head high in the most dignified manner he could manage.

"I have no idea as to what he's going to do now. The Sultan of Sulfur Dioxide won't be too amused by an element performing tricks and dancing around in a sombrero," said Caspar Calcium, nervously scribbling on Xerxes' cape.

"Stop that, you incompetent fool. No one touches the royal attire of the noble gases," yelled Xerxes Xenon, brushing the chalk from his cape and glaring at Caspar who desperately sought shelter in the pouch of Jeanne-Marie's kangaroo.

In an explosion of purple, Io Iodine slashed at the Sultan with a glimmering golden machete causing a streak of violet to slice through the Sultan of Sulfur Dioxide. "Where'd he get that sword from?" asked Jeanne-Marie, staring in disbelief at the battle being waged within their kitchen.

"It's not a sword. It's called a machete even though it resembles a sword," corrected Xerxes Xenon. "All members of the halogen family are capable of creating a mystical weapon. He won't last for long though. The Sultan is too powerful."

"He's weakening him though," said Ollie Oxygen. "Io Iodine is beginning to combine with some of the Sultan's sulfur elements weakening the power of the remaining sulfur dioxide elements. Quickly, follow me. We have to neutralize his acid rain army. That may be enough to cause him to flee."

"Good idea," said Xerxes, staring at the explosions of violet and yellow streaks erupting from the two dueling molecules. "The Sultan of Sulfur Dioxide will flee if he doesn't have enough power to destroy everything in his path. We may not be able to completely annihilate him but we can smash his army."

"Uuuuggh, wake that sleepy Eugene Europium," said Caspar Calcium, gazing at Eugene who comfortably rested in the gardenias. Grabbing Eugene Europium by the hand, Caspar Calcium and the others raced through the backyard towards a billowing mass of yellow cloud-like creatures. As the group neared the sulfur dioxide army, a mist of acidic rain shot towards them.

"Aaaaah, I've been hit," screamed Eugene Europium, plummeting towards the ground. Landing with a thud, Eugene Europium crumpled into a heap. The Sultan's henchmen surged forward unleashing a stream of acid.

"Xenon," roared Xerxes, firing a blinding green beam into the sinister henchmen of the Sultan.

"Oxygen," shouted Ollie, emitting a dazzling blue stream from his clenched fist. The element guardians' brilliant streaks momentarily knocked the menacing warriors backwards. Quickly recovering from the blow, the sulfur dioxides unleashed another torrent of acid rain forcing the elements and the two girls to dive for cover.

"Save Eugene," screamed Jeanne-Marie, staring at the crumpled, motionless figure of Eugene Europium.

"We're going to try," assured Ollie Oxygen. "First, we have to stop the Sultan's henchmen. Caspar, aim a blast of your chalk powder at the warriors. If we can create a lime molecular haze, we should be able to neutralize those devilish fiends."

"Sounds good to me. I think a lime base will definitely neutralize their acid," exclaimed Caspar, grasping his tooth firmly with both hands. "By the power of the elements, I summon calcium," chanted Caspar Calcium. With a sudden flash, the air became engulfed in a flurry of white specks.

"Oxygen," yelled Ollie, shooting a blast of shimmering blue into Caspar's white powdery mist. A glimmering white, boiling solid engraved with the letters CaO swelled for a moment before surging into the midst of the Sultan's legions. Scattering wispy fragments of the yellow cloud-like soldiers, the lime absorbed not only the acidic mist but the remaining sulfur dioxide warriors as well. The green grassy lawn rapidly became drenched in a thin layer of white powder. Silence fell over the yard where moments before the clamor of a vicious battle had permeated the air.

"Noooo......" screamed a hideous mass of yellow light, shattering the momentary silence. "You will never escape the fury of the Sultan. I will return," threatened the Sultan of Sulfur Dioxide, vanishing into the blue morning sky.

"¡Hola, amigos!" greeted an exhausted yet cheerful Io Iodine, resuming his original shape. "¡Fiesta tiempo!" shouted Io Iodine, tossing his sombrero in the air.

"It's definitely time for a party, my little Spanish friend," agreed Xerxes Xenon, grabbing Io Iodine by the shoulders and dancing merrily about the yard.

"What about Eugene Europium?" asked Jacqueline not in the celebrating spirit as long as her friend remained motionless in the middle of the yard.

"Oh, he's not hurt. He fell asleep when he hit the ground," said Ollie Oxygen, patting Jacqueline on the head. "Everyone's in great shape. Look at Xerxes. He isn't even acting noble or pompous."

"Girls, what are you doing playing in the yard in your pajamas? Get in here, right this minute," scolded the girls father, standing on the porch. "Who got detergent all over the yard?"

Trying hard not to laugh, Jacqueline followed her younger sister into the house. Neither of the girls uttered a word. They knew their father would calm down in a moment. The elements and their adventures would remain the children's secret — for now.

Don't Miss
The Next Exciting Episodes of the
Adventures of the Elements
in
Rings of Enlightenment

Crossing through the dreaded Valley of Forlorn Isotopes, Catherine and her brothers and sisters help the element guardians in battling sinister isotopes in a life and death struggle to reach the Palace of Knowledge. Reaching and discovering the secrets of the Palace of Knowledge is only the beginning of the children's journey. After receiving a mysterious gift from the Great Ones at the Palace of Knowledge, the small group of elements and children take a wrong turn on their trip home and land in ancient Greece where they are captured by thieves, separated, and sold as slaves. Will this weary band of travelers escape their cruel slave masters and reunite in time to find the portal home or will they be trapped in ancient Greece for life? Only the bravest and most cunning human guardians dare venture into the terrifying dangers lurking within the Rings of Enlightenment.

Be a Guardian!

Don't miss a thrilling chance to save the world! Bring Home ADVENTURES OF THE ELEMENTS

$4.95

Look for future Adventures

1s

Embassy Court Productions, PO Box 608, Beaumont, TX 77704

Please send me a copy of *Adventures of the Elements*. I am enclosing $_____
(Please add $2.00 for shipping and handling. Include $0.50 for each additional book. Do not exceed $5.00.)

Send check or money order - no cash or C.O.D.s please.

Name _____

Address _____

City_____ State/Zip _____

Please allow four to six weeks for delivery. Offer good in the USA only.

Price subject to change.